Father of

12 THINGS TO HA
THE TITLE OF THIS BOOK

1. The first Health Club (Gym) to embrace the multi-purpose concept of weight-training, squash, exercise to music (later aerobics) bodybuilding, sauna, spa, restaurant, beauty salon and crèche.

2. The first National Weight-training Instructor Course with over thirty thousand students qualifying to work in the industry.

3. Writing the book *The Gym Business* – the first of its kind in the UK.

4. Being a part of forming the NVQ for sport and recreation.

5. Co-founder and Chairman of the Fitness Industry Association.

6. Winners of the government National Training Award.

7. Named the Multi-marathon man by BBC Television for my solo attempt from John O'Groats to Lands End.

8. Competed in 26 marathons, five world masters championships, ran 126 miles in one day and achieved a 2.31.50 at the London marathon at the age of 45.

9. On my 40th birthday I ran forty miles, lifted 40,000lbs in forty minutes, played four people at squash and completed 400 consecutive sit-ups.

10. On my 50th birthday I ran fifty miles, lifted 50,000lbs in fifty minutes, played five people at squash and completed 500 sit-ups.

11. At the age of 75 climbing in the Swiss Alps.

12. Three Lifetime Achievement Awards in three segments of the industry:
    - 1997 – Life Fitness – Distinguished Service Award – Fitness Industry Association
    - 2005 – The Oscar Heidenstam Foundation – Outstanding Contribution to Physical Culture.
    - National Fitness Awards 2011 – Lifetime Achievement Award

DEDICATION

This book is dedicated to my wife Brenda and all my family.

Simon: There is always a way. Keep going Best Wishes

Ken Heathcote

Published by Ken Heathcote
Publishing partner: Paragon Publishing
© Ken Heathcote

The rights of Ken Heathcote to be identified as the author of this work have been asserted by him in accordance with the Copyright, Designs and Patents Act of 1988.

ISBN 978-1-78222-149-4

Book design, layout and production management by Into Print
www.intoprint.net
+44 (0)1604 832149
Printed and bound in UK and USA by Lightning Source

CONTENTS

ACKNOWLEDGEMENTS   4
PROLOGUE   5
THE MATTERHORN   6
FALLOW STREET   19
CHARACTER BUILDING   27
GATGUNS – KNUCKLE DUSTERS – FLICK KNIVES AND GANGS   29
THE KINGS HALL   31
1st PARACHUTE REGIMENT   37
AFTER DEMOB   43
CHANCERY LANE   47
BANK STREET   49
FOOLISHNESS AND FORTUNE OR LUCK   54
SUITS AND SOCCER   57
TIME AND PLACE   61
MAWDSLEY STREET   63
MOMENTS OF MAGIC – THE SOCIAL CALENDAR   80
RUNNING MARATHONS AND MARATHON RUNNERS   83
YOU TOO CAN HAVE A BODY   95
THE 40TH   107
ARE YOUR STAFF QUALIFIED?   116
TRAINING THE TRAINERS   120
THE RE-BRAND   123
INSPIRATIONAL MARIANA   128
THE NVQ   131
JOHN O'GROATS   133
THE DAY BEFORE   139
THE PREP   150
JOHNSON FOLD AND 50th BIRTHDAY   155
THE KEN HEATHCOTE YOUTH APPEAL   160
THE 50TH   163
TRAINING INTO OLD AGE   170
DRUGS   176
STEROID USE – THE PITFALLS   181
CASE STUDY – STEROID FEVER   182
MOTIVATION   183
HOW IT ALL BEGAN – FAMILY – PRICELESS   191
EPILOGUE   201
PROGRAMMES FOR MARATHON RUNNING   203

ACKNOWLEDGEMENTS

MY SPECIAL THANKS to my wife Brenda for her infinite patience and support, not for just the typing of this book, but for all the idiosyncrasies of the past fifty-eight years and her perseverance without parallel.

My gratitude to my neighbour James Hartnell, who proofed, edited, advised and steered me through the writing of the manuscript. A coach, coaching a coach – his skill, knowledge and continual assurance went way beyond my expectations.

My thanks to all who rekindled the memories and for providing the information I thought was long gone. This was regenerated with photos and statistics that sparked and lit up some magical times of the forgotten pasts of weight-lifting, bodybuilding, running, squash and socialising that all revolved around the people, places, events and incidents that were a rich time in our lives.

My gratitude to those who contributed with their views of what our club meant to them. Lorraine Carey, Eileen Thomasson, Steve Keer, Sharon Evans, and Mariana Miskell: Their unbounded enthusiasm and endearing affection for the club and the part it played in their lives. For all of our friends who we called members, but in reality became a part of our life.

My thanks to Andrew Warner who without any prompting set up and organised a reunion for members and staff – I must also give a mention to the people who have now passed on and who took the risk to join us as members and staff in a very rocky and uncertain employment: Martha Hardman, Martin Gallagher, Bert Loveday, my Dad and my Auntie Martha who lent me four hundred pounds to help pay off our mortgage to start our club in Mawdsley Street. They were all pioneers of our business and without that early faith the adventure would never have got off the ground.

Finally, my personal gratitude goes out to Dougie Farnworth for his time, effort, unwavering commitment and the unselfishness of putting in the financial backing to make the John O'Groats event happen which hundreds will remember for many years to come.

PROLOGUE

SIX TIMES WORLD Squash Champion Jonah Barrington was once hailed as the fittest man on the planet: on this particular day Jonah and I were on court and he was showing me how to hit the ball. It sounded simple, racquet, ball, ball and racquet meet and that's it, but of course it isn't! Just like golf, tennis, badminton, soccer or any game that requires fluency, timing, trajectory or anything called skill, it is both elusive and difficult to acquire. Talent is peculiar: it has a special quality of enriching those who receive it without diminishing the ones who pass it on. And so it was for Jonah and me. For all my effort and love of the game, I would never have the particular talent that other people absorb without too much apparent sacrifice.

This is a story of a different kind of talent and the ability to make it work through perseverance, a dogged determination and a cockeyed crazy kind of optimism. Put these together and you have a recipe for another form of success or achievement.

I was thirty-four years of age when I discovered I had a measure of ability that would give me great satisfaction in life. The opening and running of Bolton Health Studio taught me about entrepreneurship, managing people and organising events. I also discovered I could run long distance and suddenly a whole new life emerged.

This book is about that: it is a story I tell often, and particularly to young people who have not yet found their vocation in life. The message is 'To keep going and to keep searching for the new you.' There is nothing new about this message: it is contained within every success story, every rags to riches story and every book written by successful people. I do not by any stretch of the imagination put myself in the rags to riches category; I just found something I loved to do and made a living doing it.

What I want most from this story is for young people who have not achieved academically or are not yet ready to settle for a humdrum life, to pick up the reins when the opportunity arises. Take the risk, just like we did and give it your all. It does not matter if you do not succeed, as long as you have given everything you have to give.

THE MATTERHORN

CLINGING TO THE SIDE of a rock face eight hundred feet up with nothing between you and the specks of dust below that you know to be people is not the most attractive place to be in the seventy-fifth year of your life.

My guide Patrick had gone on ahead to secure the rope for the final thirty metres of our climb leaving me to ponder on the isolation, stillness and eerie silence, broken only by the light breeze rustling the foliage and birds nesting in the crevices around me.

Climbers talk about the religion: the out of the world experience, detached and away from everything, just you and the rock. For this brief moment I was absorbing the two things climbers tell of; the edge of oblivion and facing it alone. From the ground I would be the fly-like creature separated only by daylight space, a solitary figure perched up above and beyond. It was then my phone rang:

'Hello this is Bolton Libraries, we have the book you ordered, can you come and pick it up please?'

Standing at a little over one thousand feet, Harrison Stickle is the highest summit in the iconic Langdale Pikes with many routes

At the age of 75 climbing the Rifflehorn in the Swiss Alps.

6

to choose to reach the top of this most distinctive mountain in the beautiful English Lakes.

One of the routes takes you up the rock face of Pavey Ark where I am now. This is a steep climb that is called a scramble. This, I was to find is a gradient of rock face that can be almost vertical. For an experienced climber or even a less experienced climber this can be a good day out enjoying a degree of challenge and the fantastic views. Running diagonally across Pavey Ark, but still a climb of some substance, is a gully of something less than a scramble on the rock face which is called Jack's Rake. These two climbs and a not too dissimilar Middle Fell Buttress were my training ground for the attempted ascent of the very renowned and spectacular Matterhorn Mountain.

My reason for climbing the most photographed mountain in the world had nothing to do with mountaineering, but everything to do with charity and stupidity: Oscar Wilde once said, 'irony is wasted on the stupid' and ironically at the age of seventy-five I had chosen the most difficult of challenges.

All this stupidity and irony started in December 2009 whilst watching a programme on ITV about the Heroes of Britain. The programme was immensely heart-warming and heart-wrenching. I sat there with tears rolling down my cheeks as I watched with equal amounts of humility and inspiration a most touching programme of all things that are human.

The programme had switched from our domestic heroes to our lads out in Afghanistan, the whole focus being centred on our boys and the tragedy of losing limbs or life, the courage of endeavour and the sad loss of the mothers of the dead. It was this tragedy that struck home the most when I listened to how the mothers had banded together to support the soldiers still out there fighting in the desert and so far away from home and family. These mothers had suffered the ultimate sacrifice of losing a member of their family and had come together as one and called themselves "The Band of Mothers." I vowed at that moment I would do something for these quite unbelievable people. What I was going to do I did not know, but I would find something.

Whilst having dinner with the family on Christmas day 2009 I vaguely recollected Paul, our son, talking about climbing a mountain in Switzerland.

'Are you still doing that charity climb?'

'Yes.'

'Is it an organised climb?'

'Yes. Why?'

'I wouldn't mind having a go, if you can fit me in.'

'I will have a chat with the others, but I am sure it will be ok.'

That was it! I was now prepared to commit to climb the Matterhorn. No analysis, no research, no idea of what to do or what it entailed, no question about ability, age or condition, just a blank sheet of paper and a blank mind. I had never done any climbing in my life, I had never even hiked since being in the army and that was fifty-three years before. This was to be an eye-opener, a mind-tester and a physical challenge (and to use the words of Rudyard Kipling) 'test my heart, my nerves and sinews long after they have gone.'

My training started 1st January 2010. I was now totally committed. The following months taught me a great deal about climbing and hiking. This kind of fitness was something new. I had to learn the basics of belaying, absailing, harnesses, clothing, footwear, helmets, ropes, knots, twin-rope systems and much, much more which at this time were all a mystery.

We all have to accept that as we become older we lose things and that is why in all kinds of sports we make allowances for age. We have the Masters in golf, shooting and archery; in athletics and swimming we have grades that allow five year increments; and at forty and fifty we compete in those age groups. With rock climbing there is no such comparison, we either do it or we don't.

To learn all the skills of climbing I had to hire coaches to teach me about the equipment and guide and lead me over the climbs of Pavey Ark, Middle Fell Buttress and crags and climbs in the Peak District. Even at this early stage I found it difficult keeping pace with the guides due to my age. There was never any question I could not do it but it was a worrying handicap.

The group consisting of Paul, Chris Hopkinson and me had hired a guide for one of our training sessions who took us up Pavey Ark before descending down to Jack's Rake. This climb meant going up the difficult side of the mountain and traversing across to a point just below the top of Jack's Rake before our descent to Stickle Tarn and ending at Dungeon Gill. This was the first time I became aware of my lack of pace and speed. Even on the downward climbs I had great problems keeping up with the other three who were all twenty-five years younger than me. Most of my indoor and outdoor climbing training was done on my own. I climbed the indoor walls at Warrington and Stockport and also the small indoor wall at Bolton Lads and Girls Club where the two coaches were a huge help. A typical entry in my diary reads:

Seven hours of heavy rain made Pavey Ark very difficult. It was an 80 metre vertical climb followed by a horizontal climb across the rock face. This section is called crescent traverse. Our guide Patrick Cave had said it was challenging. I thought it was arduous, painful, difficult and extreme, but then settled for 'potty.' The traverse took us to Jack's Rake and then back down to the Tarn at Dungeon Gill.

The seven hours of heavy rain left me sodden and exhausted but now I was learning what mountaineering was all about. This was my third attempt at learning what was needed for the climb on the Matterhorn. I had previously scaled Raven's Peak and Middle Fell Buttress, both vertical climbs of 3,000 ft, and again in the pouring rain.

The next six months were spent preparing for the climb up the Matterhorn. I trained every single day for five, six and seven hours at a time doing some form of physical effort – hikes – climbs – weights – swimming – skill training, anything that would take me that extra bit forward to get me in shape for the climb. From a very stable weight of just over eleven stones I dropped about twelve pounds. I knew I had balanced my training just right but there were still some misgivings on the time span. Another six months would have been ideal, but time was not on my side and I felt I could not be any more ready. The time had come, Switzerland beckoned, and five days of preparation in the Alps before climbing the face of the Matterhorn.

Our arrival in Zermatt we were greeted with heavy rain, not a good sign: rain meant there would be snow on the upper levels of the Matterhorn and a snow-covered mountain means 'no climb.' However, we still had another five days and the weather can change by the hour.

We later met up with our Swiss-born Italian guide Gianni who would prove to be a guide of some quality. He appeared to be in his early forties; a quiet bearded man with a soft accent, fluent in five languages and who spoke in a very reassuring voice. Before the start of our adventure we had a relaxed meal followed by an early night. Gianni's instruction to us for Sunday was to just go out and hike! Our first day climbing would start on Monday.

That first hike proved to be an eye opener, even over the first few miles and at the early levels of altitude I was struggling to keep pace with the three fifty-year olds; Zermatt is at an altitude of 5,127 feet with a starting point higher than my training ground in the lakes. I started to struggle at about 8000 feet. It's a funny thing this altitude, it immobilises both the limbs and the brain! Stuart and Chris were well ahead, but Paul, noticing I was struggling, stayed behind to offer support. The snow- covered mountain and what should have been a special experience was turning into a nightmare. I could not understand why my legs would not move and my stomach and bowels were turning to liquid – my head and my feet seemed to be in conflict with each other.

'I'll just take it easy, you carry on and get the coffees in.' It was Chris and Stuart who went on ahead saying they would get the coffee and apple strudel. I continued along at a snail's pace with Paul.

I have competed in 26 marathons, run over 120 miles in 24 hours and run consecutive days averaging over 70 miles per day and run myself into all kinds of physical states, but never have I experienced this kind of distress. This was just my first day and usually when the body starts to say this is too much, the mind takes over and makes adjustments. I had felt the fatigue coming on for about an hour and then in the space of just a few minutes the whole system started to shut down; this wasn't just tiredness or even exhaustion, it was something I had never encountered before. Everything all around me on the mountainside seemed to be happening in slow motion. There was a scattering of people, a couple of hikers, someone up ahead on a mountain bike; I could see a vague shape of the station where the Gromergrat Railway Track came to an end and beyond that the restaurant and mountain retreat which was still half a mile away.

The next half hour was like walking in thick gluey treacle, but slowly, ever so slowly I managed to reach the mountain road that led to the station and a few minutes later the buildings and the loos! I spent twenty minutes or so before joining Stuart, Chris and Paul in the café with no appetite for either the strudel or coffee, opting instead for nothing else but a mouthful of water.

Chris pointed to the strudel, 'You won't be wanting this then?'

'No thanks,' and with that they cheerfully devoured the lot.

Paul and I made the return journey to Zermatt on the train, a downhill journey of about forty minutes. As we disembarked we could see our guide Giovanni in the café across from the station and miraculously I was already beginning to recover. I think the descent of about

5000 feet was obviously helping. Traditionally, our group would had a drink with Gianni and yes, I even managed a beer.

The following day was our first high altitude rock climb and for some reason I had no fear that I might once again feel the tiredness experienced today. When we were half-way or at the top of a rock face with the feeling of – 'this could be it', Gianni was the person you would want to have on the other end of the rope. God only knows what was going through his mind when he was dragging me up that precipice!

With my appetite improving, we went out later in the evening to eat at a local Pizza place, but it had not recovered enough for me to try the apple strudel.

The Via Ferratas date back to the nineteenth century and are strongly associated with the First World War. They were first built in the Dolomites to aid the movement of troops. The one we were about to climb was specifically built to help the people of Zermatt to scale the mountain separating Switzerland and Italy during the Second World War. Zermatt's Mamutt Via Ferrata towers above the town and consists of a mixture of ropes, cables, pegs and ladders in vertical and horizontal climbs.

We climbed for approximately two hours after a forty minute hike to the base of the rock face. The object of this exercise was to find out if we had any reservations about height. The Mammut Via Ferrata consists of tough scramble climbs with all kinds of different challenges. For example, there is a wire-built ladder that takes the climber to the peak of the climb: this ladder is about twenty feet long and eight hundred feet above the town below. Getting to this ladder finished the days climbing. we were aided by iron rungs (stemples) pegs, carved steps, ladders and even bridges! This enables the relatively inexperienced to enjoy dramatic positions and access difficult peaks which are normally the preserve of the experienced climber.

It would appear that at one point I would unwittingly create some drama! At about seven hundred feet I had failed to hook up to the fixed rope. Both Paul and Chris became aware of this mistake – one slip and I would fall to who knows where. I was told later by Paul the first thing to come into his mind was 'How do I explain this to my Mother?' That one metre of being unassisted and unsupported brought me close to a perilously undignified exit and close to extinction. But, like the ancient crippled cat, the three feet three inches of rock face was negotiated successfully.

11

'What's the fuss?' I said, while everyone around me were close to having a heart attack.

It was early afternoon by the time we had scaled the Mammut Via Ferrata and we had gone from ground level to about 8000 feet. I had no tiredness from yesterday's ordeal, no sense of altitude (which normally starts at about 6000 feet) and none of the symptoms I had experienced the day before. What I did notice was how much slower we were on the hike with Gianni constantly preaching rhythm – rhythm on the hike and rhythm on the climb. I immediately identified this with running marathons and distance swimming: both of these events are all about consistency, perpetual motion and being relaxed even when under pressure: rhythmic in movement with the pulse working in tandem with a given distance and time. Gianni would prove to be not just a guide, but an interesting, much informed and experienced coach.

I don't know if all the guides were of the same quality as ours, but we spent hours in total isolation climbing and hiking with Gianni and rhythm and pace made sense when at altitude. Unlike the first day on that first climb, I would never again suffer from the bodily conditions I had experienced. I asked him about fluid and diet which is a pet subject of mine. He said, 'Just tea the night before, ordinary food and maybe an occasional beer.' When we stopped to have a sandwich and a coffee out of a prepared flask Gianni would sit quietly, but if offered he relished a piece of the many Marks and Spencers Swiss chocolate bars that Brenda had packed in my luggage to take on the climbs.

On one occasion Chris asked Gianni if he still enjoyed guiding clients on the climbs and his reply, looking straight at me, was, 'Only when I have a seventy-five year old who has never climbed before.'

This was a huge time of learning and a time to test ourselves. Mountaineering is a scary, scary skill to administer. Even at our level the really difficult climbs are not attempted. The danger is always there! A fall of twenty or thirty feet can be crippling or fatal. The professionalism of these guides is phenomenal – all risk is at a bare minimum: no chances are taken, yet a simple slip can end it all. On more than one occasion one of us would slip, it would just be an incorrect placing of a foot or hand and the precautionary rope or harness would take over and correct the risk. The greatest fear is fear itself, but providing you abide by the rules you should not come to much harm. Well that is what I kept telling myself.

I talked to many people who climbed. Many of these were seasoned lifetime climbers and every one of them said the same: it's about living on the edge, being professional and overcoming the fear, but without question fear is the dominant factor and the stories that came out of these talks would reinforce these beliefs. Even the most experienced of climbers will get the flutters when viewing a prospective and difficult climb. The battle with nature is never easy.

Just what was going on in Gianni's mind we will never know: we were scheduled to attempt our climb of the Matterhorn on the Friday and the weather was not favourable. The Matterhorn is hugely picturesque with its towering structure isolating it from the surrounding landscape and we had not even had a glimpse as yet of the cloud-covered mountain that dominates the town of Zermatt.

The sheer climb from a relatively flat surround to 15,000 ft is by its own nature un-hikable. It is a high grade scramble over a snow laden rock face. If the snow continued to fall we would not be able to test our stamina and skills. However, the weather in this part of the world can change by the hour, so we continued our build-up for the climb. The next day's climbing would present us with many challenges.

The Rifflehorn is quite simply a climber's paradise: good rock, fantastic views and easily accessible. It's a great training ground for bigger exploits and climbs like the Matterhorn and is considered to be one of the best climbs anywhere.

Our day started by catching the train in Zermatt for the ascension to Gonergrat before disembarking at Rolenbode. We then had to follow the well-worn path to the base of the rock. The Rifflehorn stands at 2928 metres or about 10,000 feet. On a clear day you can see the Gorner Glacier and looking across the glacier you can see the immense alpine wall of the Brierthorn's North Face – a peak we would be climbing later in the week. To our left was the Monte Rosa and to the right the Matterhorn. These stunning views would be restricted until we had climbed to the peak of the mountain. Written in the blurb for prospective climbers it says, 'It is hard to imagine a rock climbing area with better views.' The views were certainly not wasted on us.

On this our third day we had two guides: Chris and Stuart would be accompanied by their guide with Paul and me being led by Gianni. Not only would we climb this mountain; we would also abseil down about 50 metres before climbing up again. I don't want to give the impression that we were now looking like accomplished climbers. We were not: our guides had obviously selected the right route for us to take. This was never said, but we kind of got that impression. When peaking out we would have an area of about 15 feet x 20 feet, plenty of room to eat our sandwiches and drink our coffee, and not forgetting the Marks and Spencers Swiss chocolate!

Just like the previous day we ended on a high, returning to Zermatt to have that traditional beer in celebration of a hard day and accomplishing what we had set out to do. Everything we do in life is a risk: but pitting your skill, fitness and limitations against the elements is really a demanding sport!

Acclimatisation

August is considered the best month of the year for climbing and although the snow was still lying heavily on the Matterhorn we could at last see some clear blue sky, so it was hoped most of the snow would go. Gianni wanted me to take a rest while he took the other three to scale the Pollock: this is a snow covered mountain without the steepness of the Matterhorn. He said, 'The long hike to reach it is not something I want you to do.' The chance to stay at altitude to get some time acclimatising was more than welcome. Paul, Chris

Paul, Chris, Stuart and me with a guide on the Rifflehorn.

and Stuart being regular skiers had all spent a great deal of time at altitude, but my plan was to take a cable car as high as it would go and stay there for a few hours.

We were now beginning to learn the Matterhorn was not so much about the height of the climb, but more about speed, as the climb to the summit and back in the daylight is critical. Everyone who takes up the challenge stays in a mountain hut overnight and starts the climb starts at 4.30am in the dark with torches to help navigate the ascent, the theory being it is easier to climb up in the dark than climb down in the dark. Whatever the reason, you have to get up to the summit and back to base-camp before nightfall. Gianni's recommendation for me to rest the day before was sound advice.

We had all risen at about 6am to follow our own ritual. We were staying in rented accommodation in a 2 bedroom chalet with facilities consisting of a lounge, kitchen and 1 bathroom with shower, so the obligatory toiletries, or as we called them in the army, ablutions, were systematically on a rota. I suppose under these conditions there had to be a discipline: Paul was in charge of the butties, Chris did the shopping. I can't remember what Stuart did, but I found my level with the washing-up or in restaurant terms, kitchen porter! It all worked pretty well and the mundaneness of the chores would set us up for whatever the day would hold.

Chris, Stuart and Paul set off with their guides and I went in search of a place to acclimatise. My choice was the cable-car that took the skiers up the Kliener Matterhorn Glacier. I found it quite extraordinary to see the volume of people embarking on ski lodges from all over the world to experience the thrill of free falling down a mountain of snow. The Kliener Matterhorn Glacier is the highest ski lift in Europe and considered by many to be the best of its kind in the world for summer skiing and training. The lodge offers food and drink, souvenirs, clothing plus all kinds of other temptations. My goal was just to stay up there and keep moving around.

The view on this beautiful sunny morning was spectacular: it seemed I had selected a day that would provide a rare treat looking out over forty peaks that were all over four thousand metres high. Dominating this panoramic view was the Matterhorn; to the west was Mont Blanc the highest mountain in Europe. Closer and just to my right was the Brierthorn: I didn't know at that moment in time, this was a peak we would be attempting in 2 day's time. This was a great vantage point. I could see a helicopter traversing across the valley below, no doubt transporting food or people skiers to another lodge on a lower slope. The 3,883 metre platform I was standing on is reached by an elevator forged out of the mountain. You then climb 10 metres up some stairs that takes you to an ice cave (glacier grotto) with fantastic views to the glacier below. It was not just a case of acclimatising and a chance to see the magnificent view; it was also a chance to see works of engineering that defy belief.

The Brierthorn

It was now becoming increasingly obvious that the Matterhorn would not be submitting itself to the marauding climbers. The protective clothing of snow would not succumb to a warmer climate and would remain impenetrable until the summer of the following year. We still had a day's climbing to do and Gianni had chosen the Brierthorn. Once more I went up by cable car to the Kliener Matterhorn Glacier, only this time it was with Gianni and Paul. We crossed the glacier before hiking up the 4,000 metre snow-covered mountain.

This is when Gianni's advice would pay back its reward; keep to the rhythm was the advice that kept us on track and on time. The snow covered Brierthorn required crampons, hiking sticks and plenty of

Paul and me at the summit of the Brierthorn with the unclimbable snow-covered Matterhorn in the background – a shared triumph.

warm clothing. This ascent would test my stamina and also my ability to deal with altitude.

The Brierthorn is located on the border of Switzerland and Italy: it lies in the main chain of the Alps approximately halfway between the Matterhorn and Monte Rosa. From the Kliener Matterhorn cable car, you have to first transverse the glacier and then gradually climb to the peak through heavy snow. This climb is considered to be one of the easier climbs but without a doubt it was our highest yet. The standard route goes from the glacial plateau before ascending to the summit. We were just three people in the middle of a chain of climbers stretching for about 200 yards with the soft deep snow drawing on our energy, but Gianni's mantra of 'Keep with the rhythm' now paid dividends.

Just behind, in the long line of mountaineers, there was a young eager foursome from Germany whose leader was eager to pass us. It was not that we were stalling: we were keeping pace with the whole string of climbers who were following the safe route to the peak. Any deviation from this route could invite tragedy with ravines, sudden drops and small ridges, all death traps just below the surface of the snow.

Let them pass was Gianni's order! Let them pass! So standing aside they strode ahead, eager and all full of the energies of youth.

'Don't worry' were Gianni's next words. 'They will come back to us.' And two hundred yards further up the climb they did! Keeping to the rhythm, we strode ahead to the summit, leaving them to try and cope with the extra demands of their oxygen levels.

There was an obvious disappointment for us all of not being able to do the climb we had worked so hard in preparing for. My mind went back to thinking of all the time I had spent in the Lake District; the endless hours of hiking locally around the landscapes of Bolton and the West Pennine Moor. The countless indoor practice at Stockport, Warrington, Bolton Lads and Girls Club, the Gym, the Pool, the Jumbles and Entwistle reservoirs. I had also been nursing a shoulder injury for weeks, a sure sign of over-exercising. In order to accommodate altitude, at each session in the pool I had practised relentlessly swimming as many as 10 individual lengths underwater, plus 70/80 lengths of the crawl. It had been a very demanding 6 months.

The real challenge however, is not the physical commitment, but how we adapt our mental state. We all have our limits, be it work, play or family; limits on our ability, our talent or lack of it; the inherited genes, our desire to make the best of what we have, in all the things we do in this precious thing called time – time that is to be used and not just filled.

The Matterhorn was not so much a challenge, but more of what next? Life and time are linear: they just go on until they stop. The attempt was just another way of using the time and the life. Another chapter in a book full of chapters that make up all our lives. Mine started 70 years ago in Fallow Street – a speck on our planet in a place called Kearsley, near Bolton in Lancashire. A dot that was to become full of the challenges of life in doing what we do with what we have been given.

FALLOW STREET

NO BALL GAMES says the sign on the gable end wall of a row of terraced houses. Nearby, the Clock Face pub stands like a beacon in the otherwise desolated area that once used to be my home. Now, the sign says it all. It used to be a place that was alive with kids playing and kicking a ball around, a place full of energy, life and laughter but that was an age ago and a world away. The year was 1940 and the street I lived in was Fallow Street, Kearsley, opposite the Clock Face pub. At the time I was five years old and the Second World War had just begun.

Fallow Street wasn't a proper street, it was a row of just six houses and we lived at No. 3. The end house was No. 1. Near to the clock face was a one-up, one down which went to a point as if the builders had run out of land and squeezed it in. Across the road we had the slaughterhouse and in between was the Anderson Shelter. I vividly remember the mad dashes to this igloo-like structure, me in my one piece siren suit, a bit like a boiler suit but warmer, where we would huddle together under blankets with flasks of tea until the all clear was sounded. Make do and mend, overcrowding and limited means were the norm but I had no recollection of being poor. Yes, our house was small and there wasn't much furniture, a table and two chairs sufficient because, as Mum told me, 'Standing up when you're eating will help to make you grow.' All the houses in those days had sticky tape on the windows to stop the glass from shattering when a bomb went off. We didn't get hit, the slaughterhouse did. The next day it was just a shell! No animals, just a place to play.

For young and old alike bombing became an almost daily part of our lives. On many occasions we would look up to see the bombers flying overhead towards Manchester and Trafford Park where the engineering and ammunition factories were situated. The Luftwaffe had ordered the bombing of civilians with Manchester City Centre being one of the targets; on many of the raids we could see the rockets called Doodlebugs or V2 Rockets. On Christmas Eve 1944 a special formation of 45 V1 Flying Bombs were aimed at Manchester, but many of the surrounding towns and villages were hit, with one Doodlebug hitting a row of terraced houses in Oldham killing 37 people. A bomb also landed in Punch Street up in Daubhill: this devastated houses all around the area leaving a crater thirty feet wide. The residents who survived the blast but lost their homes went to live with relatives or friends and were given an allowance of five shillings for the adults and three shillings for the children.

Our staple diet was bread and milk called pobs, sugar butties and tinned salmon from Canada that Mum used to mix with bread to make it go further, so we had bread spread on bread. We would have a rare piece of chicken, and in our stocking at Christmas there would always be an apple and an orange. One thing I clearly remember is having Dad's boiled egg on a Friday. I was thin and undernourished; in fact, I wasn't allowed to wear clogs because my ankles were too thin, but I never felt deprived. Rationing was with us for another five years but we were just one family amongst millions. We had linoleum on the floors and a home-made rug in front of the coal fire. Like most of the houses, the stairs were in the back room and when the coal was delivered the coalman tipped it under the stairs. There was no backyard and the toilets were at the end of the street – three toilets in a brick built building with no running water and shared by the six houses – no locks on the doors so it was advisable to sing when you were sitting.

The Golden Age of Radio and Bug Huts with High Sounding Names

Even in those dark days there were lighter moments and escapism. One of the closest of our companions was the radio; in fact it was the age of sound. It was said that Winston Churchill mobilised the English language and put it to war. The radio was a source of information and an incredible way of bringing laughter, suspense and jaw dropping stories to the nation. It would bring us live commentaries on the war time activities, a bit like the TV of today, but without pictures. The Battle of Britain reports of dog fights between our Spitfires and the German Messerschmitts were a running commentary on the blitz and other confrontations.

The radio for me was all about the live comedy shows; 'Old Mother Riley', 'Itma' and 'Over the Garden Wall' all epitomised the war years.

The golden age of radio was a life-saving medium of the war. Farnworth born Hilda Baker's perfect timing and bumbling dialogue would have us in stitches; Flanagan and Allen singing their signature tune of 'Underneath the Arches' reflected the war-time mood, just as Arthur Askey's rendition of the Bee Song opened with 'What a wonderful thing it is to be a healthy grown up busy busy bee.' It was also the time when Vera Lynn sang 'We'll meet again, don't know where don't know when' – and there was also the ground breaking sound of Glenn Miller and the Squadronaires.

The creepy stories from the 'Man in Black' would have us rooted to the hand-made rugs as did a programme on the 'Invisible Man.' Even more creepy the double act of Peter Brough, a ventriloquist, who with his dummy Archie Andrews, flashed their gags and humour across the airwaves – yes, even in those dark days of the forties we still had ventriloquism on the radio.

Later and still in the golden age of radio, we were treated each night to Dick Barton Special Agent, a nightly fifteen minute serial programme that would delight and scare you simultaneously; hot cocoa at the ready before going to bed. No TV, no Corrie, no I pods or internet, just family, a coal fire, the home-made rug and the sound of the radio being carried to the hungry ears of a rapt audience.

The Orchestra leader at the Grand Theatre on Churchgate in Bolton was called Joe Hill; Mum and Dad used to take me there every Monday and we always had front row seats in the stalls. Joe Hill obviously took a liking to us and I was regularly given his conductor's baton to wave around as though I was conducting the orchestra.

The artistes were called 'turns' and most could be heard on the radio with some of them being seen in British films. Rob Wilton, Old Mother Riley and Archie Andrews (with the suit we could now see) were just a few. After the show we would call at the UCP on Bradshawgate, a restaurant that was also fronted by a shop selling its Tripe, Cow Heel, Lamb and Meat dishes. Not being a lover of meat I would usually have chips and peas. I always thought United Cattle Products was a funny name for a restaurant.

As I got older, I would go to the pictures with a lad called Arnold Bentley. There were five cinemas in Farnworth – The Ritz – The Hippodrome – The Empire – The Savoy and The Palace – all 'bug huts' with high sounding names! Wooden seats, floors and the light from the rattling projector catching the smoke from the 'ciggies.' If it was an X rated film we would ask a grown-up to take us in with them.

'Aye give us thee money lad' would be the reply – strangers accompanying young lads is something we do not see today.

John Tommie was the nickname of the Scout Group the '1st

Farnworth.' I was not old enough to be a Scout so I joined the Cubs. We never heard the word paedophile being used but the two chaps in charge would have us all in a race to see who could get undressed and dressed again in the fastest time! Funny thing really, but it seemed to be accepted; no doubt if they had overstepped the line they would have got clobbered. Common law was not like today; this was a time when being 'gay' was against the law. Freddy Gorton, a well known figure about the town, dyed his hair and dressed flamboyantly and a man called Highway would pay lads to take a ride with him in his car. All this was done in plain sight of people and didn't seem to faze them too much – just different!

War-time was a time of small families, a big change from the pre-war years. Mother was one of 10 children with two of those dying at birth or just a little after. The Grifins were second generation Irish. Mum's dad John, my Granddad Griffin was a big Irishman with a twenty inch neck. According to family legend he was a very quiet man with very little to say. He would say 'Hello' and 'Ta Ra.' Grandma Griffin was much the same, but both were very kind, welcoming and hospitable and in spite of the poverty they both lived to be quite old. Grandma lived to be seventy-seven and Granddad, in spite of being knocked down by a bus in the sixties, lived to be eighty.

Ken, cousin Frank Finlay and Brenda at the Pack Horse Hotel Bolton.

In the thirties and forties a lot of families lived in the same street occupying four houses all two doors away from one another: this could be said of my family. There was Uncle Tommy, Auntie Ada, Auntie Maggie and Auntie Bertha. I don't know how true the story is but they told me that their Great Granddad had been kicked out of Ireland for the illicit distilling of whisky. It sounded a good story. Auntie Maggie was married to Josh Finlay who was the swimming coach for the Farnworth Swiimming Club. I suppose I should thank Uncle Josh for a good part of my fitness for like all good coaches he would preach about the power of repetition and say 'Let's do another twenty lengths.'

Well I am now into my late seventies and still doing those extra lengths and repetitions in the pool, and yes, still doing 60-70 lengths. Auntie Maggie and Uncle Josh would have three children, Kathleen, Bernard and Frank. They were all good swimmers. Frank would grow up to be a famous actor making over eighty films and television programmes. He was well know for the starring role in the TV programmes 'Casanova' and 'A Bouquet of Barbed Wire' and just like me Frank has shown his backside on TV; this happened during his filming of Casanova. With me it was during the 'Long Run' and I guess not a pretty sight in either case.

The Heathcote side of the family were a different kettle of fish and could be very vocal. My memory of Granddad Heathcote is vague: he returned from the Second World War a broken man after spending four years in a German POW camp which he steadfastly refused to talk about. My Dad used to talk about him and one of the things he told me was he wore clogs! On retiring to bed at night he would leave them at the bottom of the stairs and at the first sign of any trouble Dick Heathcote would run downstairs, jump into his clogs and go outside to sort it out. In those days clog fighting was a means of making a few bob and apparently he was good at it! He would teach my Dad to box and those early lessons earned him the right to go on and fight as both an amateur and a professional. Granddad was to die at the age of 50, a life cut short by the ravages of war.

The one thing that sticks in my mind is how they accepted their position in life. Grandma Heathcote known locally as 'Mattie' was the total opposite of Grandma Griffin. Mattie, just like her husband Dick was a fighter; so it is of no surprise that my Dad would grow up and become a boxer, and strange as it may seem he was still a very quiet and private man (except of course when he was fighting.) The thirty years he spent working out in our club Bolton Health Studio and also helping out when necessary with duties would be a rich part in his life. He had a great rapport with our club members earning him an enormous amount of respect. It is now twenty years since he was a part of the set-up but he is still remembered with affection by many people.

Grandma Heathcote had four children; My Dad, Auntie May, who tragically died of meningitis at the tender age of 28; Auntie Martha, who would join us at the club and be employed to work as an instructor with our older members. Then there was Uncle Bob, my favourite; this I suppose is due to him being a very good footballer, who, during war-time played for Queens Park Rangers and a couple of other clubs. He also was a talented boxer and an all-round athlete. I think what really appealed to me was that he had been a Commando in the Army and he was every young boy's hero.

I still have fond memories of all my relations: Grandma Heathcote always brewed me a coffee, brewed in the old way in the pan, grains rising to the top and then having to wait whilst they sank to the bottom. There was always a pinch of salt added plus milk and sugar. At the time we had no packaged food and a low salt consumption, but for whatever reason, that coffee always tasted good.

Dad got his back broken in the pit just two days before the announcement of V.E day; so whilst the world was celebrating the end of the war my Dad was beginning the fight of his life. There are no recollections of tragedy; perhaps at the tender age of nine it somehow didn't sink in. To me Uncle Bob taking me to Grandma Heathcote's on his bike seemed like a bit of an adventure – what is the tragedy? At the time Mum was pregnant with my sister Pat who would be born on the 18th July and celebrate the same birthday as me but nine years later. This resilience must be inbred: a desire to survive, survive the war, the pits and the poverty. My Dad would never go back in the mines even though we were short of money. We had our council house, our family and somehow that seemed enough.

The bike ride with Uncle Bob to my Grandma's would now become my new home for the duration of Dad's recovery. New Bury and McDonald Avenue was to be as much my home as our house in Crescent Road, Kearsley where we had moved only a few weeks before. But it didn't matter where I was as long as I was with family!

There was a huge difference to how it was then and how it is now. People never locked their doors as there was nothing to steal; we had very few material things – no car – no TV – no computer – not many comforts, but we had each other.

Arriving at my Grandma's there was no question of why or what is wrong? There were no telephones so communication was limited; we would just arrive and it didn't seem to matter. All I can think of was resilient! We had an incredible resilience. This may have been due to the time, the poverty, the war, or just a matter of: Who can I turn to? Who is to blame? What do I do now? We just got on with it! After my breakfast of pobbies I would think nothing of walking miles and being out all day with only the darkness or teatime luring me back home. I would spend a lot of time with Grandma Heathcote in the council house where she lived in McDonald Avenue, New Bury, Farnworth.

Two doors up lived the Fox family who had a daughter called Sheila. She was younger than me with short dark hair and skinny like all the kids at that time. One morning whilst on her way to school she went missing, she just disappeared, no signs, nothing, never to be seen again. One minute she was there frozen in time, the next minute gone! How can that happen? For months after her disappearance there were

Ken and his sister Pat in 1945.

25

photos of her everywhere, on lamp posts, in shop windows and even on the cinema screen. Police were knocking on doors and searching gardens, hiding behind trees just watching, waiting.

This area of Farnworth was very poor with not a lot going for it and 70 years on it is not that much different. Successive Governments have made promises, but nothing much has changed. Poverty is not about money, it's about being able to see, to see things can be different and to see that they can change.

Seventy years on, I sometimes re-visit my roots in New Bury, Kearsley Estate, Openshaw, and the Black Horse, Farnworth – you will still find the same councils who lack the vision and strength of character in accepting their own inevitability and responsibility in the spending of the nation's money. There has been little change, the grass is still uncut, there are broken fences and I find it totally demoralising.

CHARACTER BUILDING

BEING A KEEN swimmer himself and wanting me to be a good swimmer, my Dad would regularly take me to the Farnworth Swimming Baths. This was of course before his accident in the Pit. He had been told at the hospital he might never recover from the back injury, but slowly and surely and with willpower he started to make a recovery; one of the first things he did was to get me back to swimming. He enrolled me into the swimming club at Farnworth Baths where the members would meet each Friday night. I must have been about eleven years old at this time and I can recall quite clearly a particular incident on one club night which I believe to this day helped to shape my character.

It was still a time of rationing, with coal just like petrol, sugar, meat and a host of other things still hard to get. On this particular night the swimming club had not got its allocation of coal and we arrived to find that not one single member of the club had changed ready to swim. The pool lay like a sheet of glass, not a ripple to be seen, with every single member of the club stood around fully clothed. Dad never forced me to do anything – he kind of led me into things. 'Let's just do one length, and then we will go for a coffee and biscuits. Just one length' he said. We changed and stood there – a scrawny kid weighing about 7 stones, a near crippled man twisted by the ravaged effects of the accident and thirty to forty elite swimmers all fully clothed looking on; Dad and me were now being given no choice but to get in and swim. To this day I don't remember hitting the water; my mind was totally focused on getting to the other side of the pool. I have rewound this incident thousands of times and the only thing I remember is pulling myself up onto the far end of the poolside – no memory of the freezing cold – no discomfort – no recollection of the twenty five yard swim and as Dad and I walked back past the elite swimmers he quietly said

'If you don't take part you don't win, so tonight you just beat this lot.'

I did not find out until he was in his nineties the reason he had such a compulsion for swimming. He told me the story of how one day he went out to play with a group of boys on the 'rucks.' This was a dumping ground for a local mine and also a death trap where the piles of waste from the coal held pools of water which the kids would play around. One day whilst playing there, a friend called George fell into the water, none of the group was able to swim and so was unable to save him and George drowned. Dad said, as he was the oldest he felt it was his responsibility and from that time on he would have this fixation for swimming.

He never had any lessons; he said, 'I just taught myself with a mixture of strokes all fused into one.' Dad would carry on swimming until he was 90; I think that but for the onset of a bladder problem and having to have a caffiter fitted he would have swum until his death at the ripe old age of nearly 97. His philosophy in life was that you could not give your children anything more valuable than time. He would stand by that belief throughout his life by taking me, my sister Pat, and later all his grandchildren to the baths and teaching them to swim. In truth, he was a lousy swimmer, but a great Dad, Granddad and Great Granddad who loved seeing us all in the water.

I would go on to compete in swimming. Later it was weight lifting, bodybuilding and running. I could never settle for just doing, I would always want to test myself and compete. I wonder so many times if it all started with that twenty five yard swim with the crippled man who would never give up. I still believe today how that affected my character and how it may just have shaped my future.

I don't think my Mum and Dad were suited to running a fish and chip shop. Whether it was the crime ridden area we lived in and me getting into trouble, not serious trouble, but for whatever the reason they decided to sell and move back to Farnworth.

GATGUNS – KNUCKLE DUSTERS – FLICK KNIVES AND GANGS

SIR KEN ROBINSON is a pioneer in child education. His speciality is encouraging and fostering creativity in schools.

One of Sir Ken's books is called 'The Element.' He says, when you find your element in life it changes everything. He also says,

'You may not find your element and you could live your whole life not knowing what you were good at.' I found mine.

In 1947, and soon after that freezing cold swim, we moved from Kearsley to Manchester. It was then I began to realise I had some organisational skills.

Dad received £1000 compensation for his broken back – WOW – and with the money he bought a chip shop on Ashton Old Road Hr Openshaw Manchester. It was neither a step up nor a step down from the Kearsley Estate, more of a step sideways. Higher Openshaw was rough! The three years we spent there are full of memories. It was a part of my life that would help to shape me.

I don't know if anyone can see themselves or others and how they are going to turn out to be, but I am sure Mum and Dad knew I would never be an academic. They told me I was the strongest lad in the class because I was always holding everyone up and I was the bottom of the class.

I remember my insatiability for sports: swimming, football and cricket. I remember earning money by returning the empty barrows back up to the allotments in Ashton under Lyne, seven shillings and sixpence paid by the barrow boys so they could go and have a pint in the pub. I remember the crime, the gang fights, the gatguns, the knuckledusters and the poverty.

At the age of eleven I also remember being in a youth club and a big lad, who seemed to be in charge, and for whatever reason, he gave me a good hiding in front of the other lads. When I got home Dad could see I was upset and he eventually got me to say what had happened. So with Dad dragging me behind him off we went back to the youth club, where he confronted the bully. I remember the lad being a bit contemptuous until Dad caught him with a perfect right hook. After that I never ever got bullied again!

Being brought up in those tough areas teaches us that life is not fair or unfair, it just is: We have to learn to duck and weave or just get out of the way.

I would learn to wrestle with some great wrestlers and later in life I joined the 1st Para's. No matter how good or tough you were there would always be the one who was tougher. No one wins when it's like this, but neither can you not fight – Dad wouldn't always be around so I learned to hold my own.

We are shaped by our families, our environment and the twists of fate that affect us all. My time in Manchester taught me how to survive. That time taught me how to fight and more importantly when not to fight. That fighting is not about fists but about character.

Our move back to Farnworth was another sideways step, but this time it would be full of hope, expectation, opportunity and a new look at life.

THE KINGS HALL

FARNWORTH AND KEARSLEY are separated by an imaginary line around the Blackhorse area. The Blackhorse is a pub and just behind was the Kings Hall. The Kings Hall used to be a cinema that showed only silent films. That cinema had now become a Gym, a gym that would forge my future.

Mum and Dad bought a house in Russell Street about 200 yards from the Blackhorse Pub. Fallow Street was about 200 yards on the other side of the border, so effectively, we had come full circle.

I think fate must have played a big part in this. It was as though I was being drawn into this place, not just because of the Kings Hall but at the time because of the people who were using this excellent gym.

In 1950 I suppose I was like a lot of other undernourished kids. I was fifteen years of age and desperately wanted to put on some weight, preferably muscle! I was still swimming and the swimming wasn't helping much, and to be truthful it didn't help much with my self confidence.

The move from Openshaw seemed to draw a line. This imaginary line was somehow making a statement that was saying 'change.'

State of the art gym.

Leaving school at fifteen caused change: I went into the building trade to become an apprentice bricklayer and like a lot of other lads I was making a wage.

I enjoyed this time in the 50's – the music of rock and roll with Bill Haley and his Comets and Elvis Presley's 'Blue Suede Shoes.' Tony Curtis with his D.A haircut. Frank Sinatra making a record called 'Take Me Home Irene' and Billy Cotton and his Band singing 'If I Knew You Were Coming I'd Have Baked a Cake.'

The people and the economy were starting to recover from the Second World War. We could go out and buy a 'Teddy Boy' suit from Weaver to Wearer – what a name that was! A suit costing three weeks wages. It would have five buttons up the front, drainpipe trousers and a tie like a bootlace.

We had Theatres, Music Halls and Saturday Night Stomps at the local Palais De Danse and The Moor Hall in Church Street, Farnworth and we also had a 14" TV in the living room.

I remember Dad buying me some weights on hire purchase, and we, together with some friends, would train in our kitchen or in the backyard in summer.

My mentor Jimmy Halliday, Olympian and British Commonwealth Champion and lifelong friend.

So it was working on the building site during the day, training and perhaps the cinema in the evening. All new – all different – a line drawn – the past gone. Fallow Street, Openshaw, gangs, fights, disruptive schools, poverty, it was just one step across that line – a new beginning at the Kings Hall.

Jim Halliday was a Champion Weightlifter. He was British Champion, Commonwealth Champion and a Medallist at the 1948 London Olympic Games. He was also a victim of the Second World War who made a miraculous recovery after being a Japanese P.O.W. in Burma. Jim came home in 1945 after being freed weighing just six stone of flesh and bone. By 1948 he was a champion, a leader and now my mentor.

In truth I almost failed before I had started. Someone had told me that Sunday morning was quite quiet at the Kings Hall Gym. At fifteen year of age I was a bit shy, but decided to give it a try.

At 9am on the dot I climbed up the old cinema stairs to what would in effect be my future. There is something a bit ghostly about old theatres and the semi-lit room confronting me was empty. I could see Barbells and Dumbbells, a Gymnast Horse, Roman Rings hanging from the ceiling, a platform on the stage where the screen had once

A school room and part of the Monaco nightclub – note the padding on the wooden bench.

been and a fully loaded barbell on the platform. There was an almost deathly stillness.

At the far end of the stage were the remnants of a piano, presumably left by the previous owner. A piano that had perhaps once tinkled out tunes to the antics of Charlie Chaplin, The Keystone Cops, Buster Keaton and Laurel and Hardy.

There Is Only Me Here

At 9 am on a Sunday morning there was something mesmeric about this musical instrument, with the whole room adopting a sepia appearance and ghost-like atmosphere. The early morning sun was filtering through a dust covered window, a surreal setting and a bit scary for a fifteen year old lad.

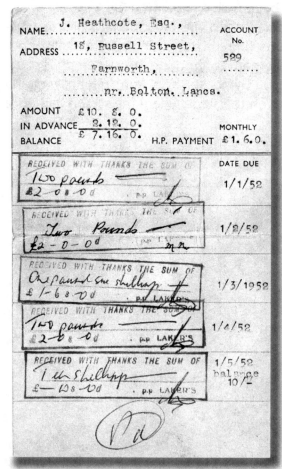

The HP Agreement for my first set of weights in 1952.

The gloomy interior of the room appeared to be playing tricks with my eyes and for a very brief moment my gaze lingered on the old piano which seemed to be moving up and down. My first thought was who had opened the doors? There is no one else here! I looked back again at the piano. Yes; it was moving, ever so slightly up and down. I thought: 'This bloody place is haunted, it's got a poltergeist thingymy.' My heart began to thump and I was just one step away from a manic retreat when someone with bag in hand joined me at the top.

That person was Joe Anderson, a seasoned weight-lifter and future mentor: He cheerfully asked

'Where is Syd?' And then said, 'There 'e is doing his leg presses.'

It was the Music Hall strong man whose photo had appeared in Saturday's paper pulling a tram through Bolton with his teeth.

"E borrows a key' said Joe. "E likes to get in early to do his training.'

Joe was a scrapper with a face like a bag of spanners from fighting the previous night, but this did not deter him from his early morning training. He was a coal miner, an Olympic lifter and stalwart of the club. Without any fuss he said, 'Let's get thee started lad, if you want to be part of us then you're welcome.'

The gym was littered with old equipment: the war years had starved the nation of everything but absolute essentials with weight-lifting equipment being bottom of the list. The mixture of Globe weights, chest expanders and a smorgasbord of forty year old Olympic bars and plates and gymnastic equipment left the whole place oblivious to how deprived it was.

I would meet champions: Jim Halliday, Syd Baker, Jack Lord and Abe Greenhalgh who would teach me the art and science of how to lift prodigious poundage and control my bodyweight so I could compete at different weights. They also taught me split second timing of the Clean and Jerk and Snatch, a technique I learned to master and an exercise that engages fifty to sixty muscles in the space of two seconds with just one repetition and more benefit than sixteen machines.

Jim's success at the 1948 London Olympic Games was testament to the rugged characters that knew no limits and scorned the deprivation.

The next four years were a magical time: a time of learning and a sense of belonging. Jim Halliday would take me under his wing and I would go on to be involved in various competitions in Liverpool, Manchester and Lancaster and across the North West.

The Kings Hall characterised the age and culture of the 50's. It would teach me far more than how to lift weights. It was a place that taught me how to forge friendships and what makes a great club, something that would come to fruition twenty years later. It was a great period.

A new wave of Bodybuilding was about to surface. This hobby would lead to people you would come to admire and value as friends.

Reg Park from Leeds set the standard and took the title of Mr Britain before going on to win the Mr Universe with John Lees from Stalybridge following in his footsteps. Closer to home I was privileged to be taught by British Champion Jack Lord and Syd Baker the 'Man in Bronze' who did a muscle control act on stage and was painted in Bronze from head to toe. His act was engineered by his sister Hilda, a famous comedian and star of stage and screen of the post war era.

The lessons learned would sink into the subconscious: the club mentality, trips, social structure, a place to meet friends, time spent teaching the skills, knowledge, techniques and workings of the human body, learning by doing. The Kings Hall offered all these but most of all it offered friendship and warmth, essential ingredients for our club of the future.

1st PARACHUTE REGIMENT

MY TIME AS an apprentice bricklayer came to an abrupt end when I had some issues with the building company. I cannot remember to this day what my disagreement with them was, but whatever it was, I was out of the protection of being exempt from conscription, and this meant my next two years would be spent serving Queen and Country.

My time with HM Forces was between 1954 and 1956. The government in their wisdom had made it compulsory for the young men of the country to do National Service.

I was drafted into the Loyals Regiment at Fulwood Barracks in Preston to do twelve weeks basic training before going to Barnard Castle in Yorkshire. I remember how hard it was, the training was tough, but not unmanageable. What was tougher and for me unmanageable was the money the army paid us. We were paid weekly, cash in hand, well except that even by the standards in those days it was slave labour. The pay dished out by the Paymaster was £1.00 one week and 50p the next – £3.00 per month. It didn't take me long to start looking for another job and that is when I started to jump out of aeroplanes.

The advice of my Sergeant when I asked about more money was to go into another mob i.e. a Corps, Signals or Physical Education. I volunteered for all three – the Para's replied first and with that in mind I got a ticket to Aldershot where I was expected to do the pre Para course. This was a gruelling two week initiation designed to test us on our level of idiocy.

All the National Servicemen would have to go through this extremely demanding two weeks with only a small percentage succeeding. Unfortunately or fortunately, depending on how you want to look at it, I passed. The Parachute Regiment is a tough Regiment and I always felt privileged to be a part of it. The two weeks pre-Para course defines your commitment: it is a test to assess your ability to exit the plane door when making jumps above enemy territory. The next step was to go to Abingdon where we trained exclusively on jumps. To my knowledge no one who had passed the pre-Para course would fail those two weeks at Abingdon.

British Army Training is the best in the world and the best of the best is training to be a Para. The training is to manage fear and it is incredibly repetitive. It is the basis of an elite demand. It constantly defines and refines. It is an exact science which taught me so much. It taught me that if you really want to do it, do it this way, using this method. Top class athletes stick to this regime, it is uncompromising and it works. There were eight jumps to be made at Abingdon – two out of a balloon and the other six out of Dakotas. My first flight in a plane was when I was taken up to a height of 1000 feet and then had to jump out!

When in combat conditions you leave the plane carrying about one hundred pounds (45kg) of equipment, ammo, food and your own particular weapon (rifle, bren gun etc.) This kit bag is strapped to the left leg and when the Chute opens you jettison the kit bag and it dangles fifteen feet below. In combat conditions you exit the plane flying at approximately 800ft and hit the ground twenty seconds later. In war the enemy are there waiting and popping us off before we hit

Earning my Wings and Red Beret.

the ground. Para training is the best of the best because it trains you for the very worst encounters. By earning my Wings and the Red Beret I would get a wage of about £6 per week. Soon after passing out as a Para, I was sent to Cyprus along with another eighteen hundred squaddies.

It was in Cyprus that we would see some active service by trying to catch a terrorist group called EOKA who were trying to get the ruling of the Greek Orthodox Church – our job was to keep the two political and religious groups apart. The island was under British rule and an island of some strategic worth. This would be appreciated more a year later just after my demob when we invaded Egypt in an attempt to seize the Suez Canal. In the meantime we were given the task of keeping the EOKA quiet

I remember spending my 21st birthday sitting on top of one of those ridges on guard with a German Mouser – a kind of Sten gun. How I came to have that I do not know, but there were a lot of things that were unexplained in the Paras. When we were not running around after the terrorists we were either back in the camp training or we were in Kyrenia – a small town with a port, a few bars, the odd restaurant and a bug hole of a cinema.

I remember going to the cinema and quite unbelievably watching a film starring Doris Day. The title of the film was 'Lucky Me' and it was

Leisure time on Snake Island in Cyprus with the squaddies.

39

in cinemascope. In the bug hut in my home town of Farnworth the wide screen had not yet been seen so we felt quite privileged. When the film was over we left the cinema to have a steak at the local eatery which was just 100 yards away: before we got to the restaurant there was a huge bang and the cinema blew up! Whoever had planted that bomb had just got their timing wrong.

On another occasion, and breaking camp orders, four of us all carrying weapons went out into the into the old city of Nicosia, an out of bounds area for the army. It never failed to puzzle me how conflict and killing does not deter us from having a good time! Why would four young men travel the mile into Nicosia to get into a threatening and alien place just to do what they wanted to do in these dens of iniquity and not care?

Entering the old town, we knew the risks we were taking. We had had a few beers and visited a few unsavoury places when someone suggested going into the Lion's Den. Without another thought we all jumped into a taxi and crossed into the forbidden area of the old town. Within a minute the taxi turned into a small square packed with people which slowed us down. If our driver was Greek or Turkish I do not know, but he obviously didn't like the situation and we weren't relishing it either. Without any further warning, a group of young men started to rock the vehicle and it didn't need a Sherlock Holmes to detect how volatile the situation had become. The kids were obviously drunk and we were now thinking that they were smelling blood.

The hundreds of hours' training that we had all gone through now kicked in. None of us said a word; all that could be heard within the taxi were four rounds being slotted into the breach. It was then I politely suggested to the driver that he should f...... well get his foot down or he would be in grave danger of losing his brains. There was no panic or hysterics, but I am sure the pulse rate was at its maximum and that every muscle and sinew was taut as the 'fight or flight' was subconsciously making its decision. These were volatile times – EOKA had done a job on us! Murder Mile was a term describing a main street in Nicosia where terrorists would gun down anyone who challenged the regime. There was no doubt in my mind that these young bucks fuelled by alcohol and religious fervour would have had no qualms of taking us out. Sensing fear for himself and for us the taxi driver had no hesitation in hot-footing it out of the square. No damage this time, but a very close shave.

The Forces are a great institution – an institution that has a very noble cause. We are living in a very troubled and complex world. There is a lot of evil in the world. There is greed, political and religious influences and territorial and strategic positioning.

The human race is by definition here to survive. Ambition, good and evil are part of our make-up. Law and order, be it on our streets, in our towns and cities or on the global stage is ever present. Four young men out of order and out of bounds were on the brink of losing out on life until the training took charge.

The British Armed Forces do an incredible job and the lads out there in Afghanistan are never far from our thoughts. They risk their lives so we have safer streets, towns, cities, and homes. The ugliness of war will be part of this world as long as there is a world; it is the price we pay for living.

Many times I felt the fear on being alone on guard in some gully, river bed or on a winding path in the midst of the Troodos Mountain ranges. Being in a twenty mile radius and caught in a raging forest fire with only the mountain village people to save us from burning. Seeing a mate blow his own brains out because of his immaturity together with all the things that we will never learn to contain until time allows us to believe in our own mortality. It isn't fair, nor is it right or wrong: it is just how life is, and we have to deal with it.

When I think back, I never realised just how valuable my time spent in the armed forces was. It is only now, many years later, that I think of how I could have made more of what I had. Being a National Serviceman in a volunteer regiment is not ideal for either the army or the squaddy. The army wants long term commitment – the conscript just wants to get it over with. The army builds a certain kind of loyalty and a certain kind of camaraderie: I remember my Dad saying how strong this camaraderie was down in the mines. They were losing people every day due to the bad working conditions with falling rock, gas explosions and inadequate equipment. The mines, like the army, were about life and death. It was also about courage and a need for people to rely on each other. The army was to be my first lesson in such qualities.

A quarter of a century later I would experience these qualities again when attempting to run from John O'Groats to Lands End and having to depend on others. The army would teach me about fear and isolation. Lying in ambush in the middle of the night on some

41

mountain track with only yourself and your imagination, and not knowing who was coming up the path.

The army is not what the ideal world wants, but in a world without too many ideals we need it.

My tenure with the British Army was about to end. The invasion of the Suez Canal was imminent and in their wisdom the army decided to send me home. I guess it would not be good publicity for National Servicemen to lose their life in the last few weeks of their conscription and I spent my last few weeks at Aldershot Barracks working in the stores.

Our Battalion 1st Paras were to do the beach invasion with the 3rd Paras doing the air drop leaving the 2nd Paras on standby. Half of me was wishing I had been there. The other half was glad to be back in the UK safe and sound. My mates Dave Crossland, Joe Smith and Fred Davies all managed to come through the ordeal and get back home. Some three years later I would meet up with Dave again when I was asked to be best man at his wedding.

Demob was more than welcome. I had not enjoyed being a squaddy. Yes, I enjoyed the experiences, the camaraderie and the chance to be part of a great regiment, but to be forced into National Service for two years went against the grain. I just wanted to get home, find a job and get back into training, but first I had to find a place to train.

AFTER DEMOB

THE KINGS HALL was long gone, demolished and now a piece of waste land. Jim Halliday had set up stall in a room over the Bowling Green Pub and a good friend of mine Bert Loveday, a former Mr Britain, had set up a club in Halliwell Road which he called The Gateway to Health, a terrific name for a gym.

The one place I would be drawn to was a gym above the Co-op in Bridge Street in Bolton Town Centre and it would be here that something would happen to change my life for ever. This gym was run by a chap called Cab Cashford: He was an ex-professional wrestler and had a face to prove it. Cab's gym was different: it was clean, had polished floors and the walls were bright and freshly painted. Cab ran a good club: it was disciplined, he had rules and commanded respect. I would train on a Monday, Wednesday and Friday as Tuesday and Thursday were reserved for the girls.

This was all new and came as a complete surprise to me. This was a bodybuilding gym with just as many women as men wanting to work out with weights. The standards set by Cab were something I

Cab Cashford's Gym 1956. Blue knickers and white tops – the uniform of the day. A far cry from the leotards and the high tech accessories of piped music, aerobics, pump, drums and enough water to get a camel across the Sahara.

had never seen before and from which I was about to learn a great deal. This would not only teach me about style, cleanliness and how people respected quality, but also it would be here I would see my future unfold and meet Brenda Walsh, who three years later became my wife.

Cab Cashford was a really nice guy: he had vision, he was disciplined and a natural matchmaker. Starting to work out in the gym at Cab's soon after leaving the army was the place I would make some lifelong friends. To mention just a few there was Malcolm (Doc) Doran, Pat and Mike McCarthy, Big Pete McDermott and Keith Williamson.

Cab organised an 'Open Day' to show the members of the co-op, from whom he rented the room what the gym was all about. The lads were to do some lifting demonstrations and even some bodybuilding posing. The girls in their white tops and navy blue gym knickers would do some calisthenics and group exercise with background music. I recall there was a balance of members both male and female. There were no mixed sessions, but the commitment to heavy training and weight lifting was extraordinary, lovely looking girls lifting heavy weights with not a muscle in sight.

Cab Cashford's Gym 1956. Back row far right yours truly. Front row 2nd from right Brenda. A time of camaraderie and lifelong friends. Big Pete McDermott, Keith (Willy) Williamson, Malcolm (Doc) Doran and Roy (Young Hack) Keats.

I must have met Brenda on that first open day but I have very little recollection of it. The week following the demonstration, Cab had organised a trip for the members to a physical culture show being held on Morecambe Pier where topping the bill would be the great British bodybuilder Reg Park. Cab's matchmaking talents would now come into force and be put to good use. I was to have been teamed up with a girl called Dorothy Kay and my mate Keith Williamson was matched with Brenda. Somehow the arrangement got confused and on the night I found myself with Brenda. A relationship that has now seen close on fifty-eight years. I had only been out of the army a few months and my future was sealed forever.

There is a saying that 'We will only have three life changing events.' I don't know if this is true, but I do know that this was undoubtedly one of mine.

Cab Cashford's still holds many memories of a great bunch of lads and girls who forged friendships. I still see Doc, Pat and Pete along with others who trained at that special gym in Bolton. Roy Keats is another, who with me, a few years later would open a small gym above a bookies in Farnworth and later, we would both take up wrestling in both amateur and professional bouts.

When Bill and I decided to open a gym in Bank Street many of the lads would come along to join and they would also follow us to Mawdsley Street. Most of them are still alive and kicking, and yes, now in their seventies, still working out on the weights.

Four years later in 1959, Brenda and I got married: our honeymoon started with a thirteen hour overnight coach trip on a Yellow-ways Bus to stay for one week at the Beachcroft Hotel in Newquay Cornwall where we had this enormous bedroom with panoramic views over the Atlantic Ocean. Bed, breakfast, evening meals and entertainment all for the total sum of eleven guineas each! An idyllic week spent in idyllic surroundings in the continuing heat-wave of that year and looking forward to a future that would be challenging, eventful and ultimately rewarding.

We returned to Kildare Street in Farnworth to the three bedroom terraced house we had bought for £1250. The bathroom was just 5ft x 7ft and consisted of just a bath and sink with a notch cut out of the bathroom door to accommodate the rim of the bath when opened. Our toilet was outside at the bottom of the yard. Our children Paul and Karen would both be born in the front bedroom of our house, delivered by the midwife and our GP Dr Gracie, a Scot who loved his golf and his whisky, and cared passionately for his patients. Always pleasant and talkative, even when called out at ungodly hours to Paul and Karen for major things like 'wind' and other natural phenomena. I would open a gym in Chancery Lane in Bolton town centre.

It is a phenomenon of nature and a constant puzzle how upheavals in the world fail to influence the individual's determination to continue to do ordinary things and to carry on leading ordinary lives.

Malcolm (Doc) Doran – No drugs, honest endeavour and still going today.

CHANCERY LANE

THE CHANCERY LANE Barbell Club was located in a cellar beneath the typewriter shop of Maxwell Jones. It covered a total area of 400sq.ft. The only running water was in the communal toilets servicing four upstairs businesses.

Pumping iron in a cellar in the early 1960's was the best that we could get. On the wall and drawn by hand were posters with motivational slogans:

'If you think you can, if you think you can't, you're right.'

'Train with a purpose'

'The Programme will only work if you work at the Programme.'

The two words of 'work' were underlined to provide some inspirational impact.

Whitewashed walls, flag floors, a blacksmith-made Lat Machine bolted to the wall, a Bench, Squat Racks, and a small amount of Barbells and Dumbbells in a room of a cellar whose lease would expire when the owners decided to find it a better use for storing paper, files or broken typewriters. The 1950/60s change and eviction were all part of the game in running a gym.

This would be the decade of the brutal assassination of John F Kennedy shown live on American TV watched in horror by millions who at the time were sitting in their homes viewing the news.

We were just a bunch of young guys expressing ourselves in a way that was special to us. For this time in the gym we were apart from the world: each repetition, each set, each exercise defining us. Pushing, pulling, lifting, and striving: just one more pound, one more inch, and one extra breath, just one more challenge with every muscle, tendon and sinew and every body part being taken to its limit. Nothing exists except you and the weight – a moment in time, and a time to live that moment.

Chancery Lane proved to be a pivotal point. The frustration of not being able to express myself was depressing. I wanted more. We had about twenty regulars training two to three times each week whilst another fifteen to twenty would come in on a casual basis.

Given the right conditions I knew we could treble or quadruple those numbers and break free from the mentality of small. My gut feeling was there could be a lot more than what we had here.

The opportunity to grow would present itself just across town in Bank Street.

BANK STREET

BANK STREET IS LOCATED on the edge of Bolton Town centre and halfway down the street is a shop called 'Joe's Lost Property' and known by everyone as 'Joe's Umbrellas.' The Proprietor of this shop is Joe Moss who is famously known for selling and repairing umbrellas, bags and travelling trunks.

To the left of the shop stood the Cromwellian Night Club and to the right was a doorway that led down a twenty metres long narrow alleyway that opened out onto a small courtyard and a three storey high building that once housed a clothing factory. Each floor of the building was about thirty feet long by fifteen feet wide. The first floor was already rented out to a couple who were selling good-as-new second-hand clothing. We rented the first and second floors and turned them into a Gym. That dark alleyway leading into that quite dilapidated building became the entrance to our new venture called Bolton Health Studio, a business lasting nearly forty years. There was no lighting in either the passageway or courtyard so to make it look lighter we lime-washed the walls, but even with this, during the winter

The first Bolton Health Studio behind Joe's Lost Property and almost a lost cause for us in the desperately hard start of the journey.

months it still proved to be quite intimidating. This building at the back of Bank Street was to be our home for the next four years – four years of unbelievable difficulty, trial and error and blind faith.

When we opened for our first year of business in 1968 and a journey into the future, it was only in the evenings. There were no professional gyms and if you were to look in the Yellow Pages Business Directory you would not find a single entry of any description for a Gym, Health Centre, Leisure facility or Keep Fit establishment that even related to working out, weight training or exercise. There were bodybuilding and weightlifting gyms but these were mostly down some back street, in a cellar, school room or youth club, nothing that resembled a professional business and not one of these small obscure thriving little gyms had a phone.

Bert Loveday's 'Gateway to Health' was situated above the Co-op Butchers, a corner shop on Halliwell Road. Cab Cashfords had long since closed and Bolton United Harriers was now both a wrestling club and also a club that entertained the sport of weight-lifting. Bolton Health Studio at 2a Bank Street would cater for both men and women's keep fit and have two things that none of the other places had – a shower and a telephone.

Our first year of opening in Bank Street was during the hours of 6pm and 10pm. This was just the same as any other club in Bolton or for

Ladies training day 1968.

that matter any other town. Weight-training establishments were for people who treated it as a hobby and not a necessity, but our determined venture to change things was adventurous to say the least. We painted walls and polished floors; we built equipment with the help of a blacksmith and a local engineering company. We lined the walls with mirrors, we had co-ordinated and coloured vinyl covered padded benches, a Vibrator Belt which was quite an innovative idea for its

Brochure and Fees.

My Auntie Martha and first paid instructress at Bank Street – working on the waist trimmer made by the local Blacksmith – as good an exercise you can do for the new core muscles.

Bill Pearl and me in 1969. Before leaving for home to the USA his last words to me were 'I think you lads are gonna make it'.

time and also a 'Tunturi' Bike that had been specially designed by the manufacturer to serve the needs of hospital-based physiotherapists, not health club clientele. What we had in the making at Bank Street was a state of the art health club far ahead of its time. We did not have a clue as to where it was going, but going somewhere, it certainly was.

FOOLISHNESS AND FORTUNE OR LUCK

WHEN THE GROUND floor became available we decided to open 'full time' – it wasn't that the Health Club market had suddenly opened up, it hadn't, but we were basing our decision on some kind of assumption which I think is called 'blind faith.' This scientific assumption was saying to me that if we opened through the day we would attract a different clientele. In the end this turned out to be right, but it was not in the way I thought it would.

The grand opening for our full time Health Club was on the first Monday of the first week of 1969. As we knew very little about marketing and advertising we had placed some ads in the Bolton Evening News which could only be described as painful. My partner Bill Stevenson and I had both come off a building site, so what did we know? The ads we used usually showed a girl or woman in a leotard and as back then there was no colour they were in black and white. The only market at this stage was Keep-fit! Slimming, diet and exercise were not really in vogue; these were a product yet to be developed, so going full time was a gamble and thinking back rather a foolish gamble which revealed itself quite dramatically on that first Monday morning in that first week of 1969.

Bill and I had made an agreement that I would run the Gym full time and he would continue to carry on throughout the day with the work in our Building Company and become involved with the Gym in the evening. The hours were incredibly long for both of us; we were not finishing work until ten in the evening. We both had young children – Bill and his wife Kath had three girls Gina, Maria and Anita, whilst Brenda and I had Paul and Karen who were aged eight and six. Even at the weekend we would be painting, sanding floors and doing whatever needed to be done.

After some research and yet another 'gut' feeling we decided it would be quite innovative and attract more than just the regular punter if we added a new fixture. This new fixture we felt would also add to the mystique of being a member of Bolton Health Studio. So we made the decision to install a 'Sauna Bath.' As we all now know the Sauna is just a wooden box of dry heat that is heated to a given temperature to make us sweat. Not aware of this at the time we then had to go and find out what it was all about. After much debate and a lot of research we came to the conclusion that we could make our own. We did this by going to a local timber yard and having box made to measure and then the wood dry kilned. Bill would then construct it and we would have a genuine Nordic Finnish Sauna – in truth the stove was an eighteen kilowatt fire with insulated bars and special stones that had some volcanic history which we had imported from a company in Finland; we now had Bolton's first sauna bath alongside our state of the art equipment and Tunturi bike, how could we possibly fail?

The first Monday of the first week of 1969 would see me there at 8.30am preparing for the onslaught of customers. The gym was spotlessly clean and the equipment ready for use with the bike freshly oiled and strategically placed. The very innovative hot box switched on and storing heat to amaze the customers. As I opened the door like some magician pulling a rabbit out of a hat, I would say yes, it is 110 degrees Fahrenheit! It was now 10am I was pumped up and ready for opening the doors, my sales pitch rehearsed – come on down folks and be prepared to be amazed!

I had spent the first hour before opening putting the final touches to the gym; it wasn't that it needed anything doing but I think paranoia had set in and I could see things were wrong that really were not wrong. I suppose the isolation of the building and the long passageway away from the main street created that separation. I was fussing around like an old hen going over the same thing again and again.

The doors were opened spot on 10am and I was feeling a little disappointed that no one was keen to start early. At this stage there was no thinking this was not a good idea. There is a fine line between blind faith and self belief and I never for one minute thought it would not work. There was a kind of immunisation about it all; just get on with it and this is what we did.

Doors open I positioned myself against the window looking down the alleyway willing the customers to come striding down the entrance – the power of positive thinking imposing itself on to the prospective clients – eleven o'clock came and went and still there was no sign of that first potential customer, the only activity I could muster to keep warm on this cold January morning was to keep moving around the room before going back to that window.

'What's the matter with everyone' I said to myself, 'Does no one want to see my state of the art gym complete with a Tunturi Bike, a Sauna and a telephone?' My mind was already anticipating a lunchtime surge of businessmen sacrificing their lunch for a workout. Well, lunch came and went, not one solitary client: one o'clock, two o'clock, five hours had passed, no phone calls, no indication. Had there been a disaster? Had the world stopped? Had World War Three started? At this stage the back of the Cromwellian Club and Joe's Umbrellas was starting to mesmerise me, a day's study in dilapidated architecture! Three o'clock came and went and then four, but just when I thought this is it, I saw some movement deep into the alleyway. Was this to be the start of an avalanche?

Galvanised into action I scurried into the reception area to hear the sound of our first day time customer making an entrance and ascending the stairs. Pen at the ready, I quickly brushed my hair; everything neat and tidy, the blank and empty signing-in sheet all ready for this historic moment. This was the moment of truth, our very first financial transaction. Three pounds three shillings joining fee and five shillings for the first week's subscription was laid on the reception desk, cash up front.

There comes a moment in our life that we will remember for ever. That first car, the first house, the graduation, the first kiss, the first cheque in a frame on the wall, a certificate for the first swim, fun run or marathon; it can be big or small, but more than anything it is carved into the very depth of our mind. £3.3.0d joining fee and five bob for his first week subscription! I hadn't taken a penny all day, but the words that came out of my mouth were,

'Dad, I can't take your money, you're my Dad.'

The words he then uttered would help define and perceptively shift the way we thought in the future. 'You take the money son, this is not a hobby any more, it is your livelihood.'

SUITS AND SOCCER

THE FIRST SIGNS that things were starting to change were quite subtle. Frank Lang was a businessman with a chromium plating company in Farnworth. He was one of the first 'suits' to start on daytime training and would become a regular with us for a several years.

Another businessman was Colin Perks, who had a cleaning company which also happened to be in Farnworth. He would also come along and join. Colin then introduced his wife to the club and over the years they became close friends of our family.

There was Jack Wane who had a chain of butcher's shops and was part owner of the Bolton Abattoir.

Frank Fletcher, a bodybuilding colleague of mine, brought in his sixteen year old son Paul who had just been signed by Bolton Wanderers.

'He is a striker' said Frank, 'He needs to be able to jump higher and build up some power.' Paul would play for Bolton Wanderers before being transferred to Burnley Football Club and go on to play for England under 21s. Forty-five years on Frank and Paul are still good friends of our family.

It would be another suit and another Paul Fletcher who would link Bolton Wanderers and us together. Bill Ridding had just stepped down as manager when he came along to see us with Paul Fletcher. Paul was the M.D. of Seddon's Plant and Engineering Company. He was an accountant by profession who obviously had some influence within the club at the time. On that cold and frosty morning in January, I remember they were both dressed in immaculate doubled-breasted dark blue pin-stripe suits, ties, black shiny shoes and dark blue overcoats. Bill Ridding's whole demeanour reminded me of Alf Ramsey, the England Manager of the 1966 World Cup, a man with great dignity and a great presence. Just what would develop from this meeting I could never envisage. But whatever we were doing must have impressed them, as two or three days later I received a call from the current manager, the legendary Nat Lofthouse, the man they called the Lion of Vienna.

Nat's reputation as a centre forward was worldwide. The thirty goals he scored for England in thirty-three appearances is a record that still stands today. Nat's career had spanned the war years, and but for the war those goals and appearances would have been greatly increased.

Nat sounded very enthusiastic and quite cheerfully asked if he could come down to use our Sauna, something he had used before in Finland whilst on international duty.

The reason for him wanting to come down was immaterial; I was just overjoyed that he was coming. Many years later in a conversation, I was told that Nat had said to Jim Conway, the youth team coach,

'Get the lads down to Ken and get him to sort out some training for them.' This was to be the start of our relationship with Bolton Wanderers, a relationship that would last for over twenty years.

The year was 1969 and Jim Conway arrived at our club unannounced with fifteen players from the junior ranks of the football club; no warning, no phone call, no letter, no agreement and no introduction! Can you imagine that happening today? Jim's arrival and my response of having to deal with all this energy was to spontaneously outline a programme to satisfy their needs. This on the spot challenge was the first workout that would pave the way for some of the biggest names in football to use our club over the next two decades. He must have been impressed, or not given a choice. I rather feel it was the former, because over forty years later I would ask Jim

'Do you remember coming to the club and bringing the youth team with you?' and without a single second of hesitation he rattled off all the names of that squad as though it was the previous day.

The names of John Byron, Eddie Hopkinson (the goalie, capped for England) Syd Farrimond, Roy Greaves, Warrick Rimmer and a young chap called Gordon Taylor who would go on to play winger and eventually become the Chief Executive of the Professional Players Association. In total there were fifteen players, and if you were to ask any one of them today, they would remember that visit, just as I do.

That subtle change in policy brought a new dimension to our club. We saw a continuous growth of business people taking time from work to come and work out in our gym.

Football may not be everyone's cup of tea but it is the national sport and often the bedrock of every town or city that has a 'Town Team.' To have their support was huge for any business. Bolton Wanderers would make our club available to all their players. Great names like Roger Hunt of World Cup fame, Frank Worthington, Sam Allardyce, Paul Jones and Peter Reid all came in to train, with the

Bolton's team of 1969.

Gordon Taylor at 18. He was brought down to train by Jim Conway and 16 other youth team players on the instructions of Nat Lofthouse. This was the start of a long lasting relationship with BWFC and still prevails today (Photo courtesy of Simon Marland).

Nat Lofthouse in 1969 when he introduced the team to Bolton Health Studio. (Photo courtesy of Simon Marland).

managers following the players. We would welcome the likes of Phil Neal, a legendary Liverpool player, Jimmy Arnfield and John McGovern and one of our greatest advocates, Ian Greaves, who put Bolton into the first division, now our premier league. For the first time in many years it was not just the players frequenting the club, it also attracted the wives, girlfriends, their families and even the directors who became part of the mix.

We now knew that this small three storey former factory was not good enough or big enough for what we thought we needed for the future. The suits and the soccer players were now telling us there was indeed a future.

Gordon Taylor today 2013 – Chief Executive of the PFA with T.S. Lowry's 'Going to the Match' A painting of the old Burnden Park.

TIME AND PLACE

OUR MEMBERSHIP WASN'T bursting at the seams. It had grown, but not to the extent of needing much more space. The real lessons we were learning along the way were seeing the market, but not knowing what was needed to open it up. One thing we were certain about was the current premises were neither big enough or in the right place.

Instinctively again, we knew it was time to move. But that was easier said than done. I had always had trouble holding on to premises, it was just the way things happened and the amateurism of running clubs as a hobby. However, what was emerging now was not a hobby, nor in truth a business, but on the verge of becoming one. This would mean a different type of commitment. During the past two years we had simply been planting the seeds and the seeds had been encouraging in showing us that things could grow into something that would flourish. We knew Bank Street would not accommodate our future and the time had come to move.

The commitment in moving across town to Mawdsley Street was extremely difficult. For a start the old annexe to the Grammar School was in a dilapidated state. The science lab was a mess of glass containers, gas pipes, equipment and vandalised furniture. The cellar was a home for vagrants who would light fires in the old Victorian boiler room. We also found it had broken drains and was rat infested. It was an atmosphere of total desolation. The top floor had a huge amount of broken windows and was a graveyard for wayward pigeons with the floor covered in two feet of pigeon dung. The former school's eighteen foot ceilings were totally unsuitable for our needs and in addition the local authority who owned the building would only offer us a twenty year lease. The 11,000 sq.ft. Building was ideally located in the town centre, but ten times bigger than any club I had ever been in. Eventually it was to cost us £50,000 a year for rent and rates, a huge building and enormous cost. Could this be a step too far or an opportunity to do what we wanted to do?

The Building was way too big for what we needed and we had no idea of how we could utilise all that space.

Ever since we had made the decision two years before to open full time I had been continuously on the look out for more suitable premises. My thoughts thinking two or three thousand square feet would be more than adequate and for the time it probably would have been. But 11,000 sq ft was scary! The building consisted of four floors, not ideal, but where else could we go. In the two years of searching we had exhausted the town's availability.

Another thing we had to contend with was access. People did not have cars to the extent of today. The criteria for attracting customers were based on where they worked and where they lived.

Where they lived was not an option, because the market was essentially too small with our target being aimed at Mr and Mrs Average. People who lived in terraced houses, a chimney pot population. Yes, we were attracting the suits, but they would only fill a small percentage of our membership. We were a working class town and our members would be working class people.

We secured the premises in August 1971 after negotiating a rent free four month period to rehabilitate the almost derelict building. We had the usual things to contend with regarding planning permission, building regulations and so forth, but in truth the local authority were glad to get rid after seven years of decay and it being empty. We were now totally committed and the start of a thirty year adventure was about to begin.

MAWDSLEY STREET

A Shift in the Sands of Time

THE BUILDING IS detached from any other in Mawdsley Street and commands a sense of respect. It's height of three storeys, a basement, large stone mullions, a giant coloured and leaded glass window with the Bolton Coat of Arms 'Sempa Moras' is one hundred and sixteen years old.

Across from the entrance is the typewriter shop that sits above the cellars that were the home of the Chancery Lane Barbell Club. It is only fifty feet away, but a million miles in what the two clubs would represent.

It would be half a century later people would write to say how Bolton Health Studio had changed their lives with a new career and new lifetime friends that had given them joy, happy memories and even changed the course of their existence.

The move from Bank Street to Mawdsley Street would signify for Bill Stevenson and me and our families a whole new life. It would take us

Bill Stevenson and me – New beginnings in 1972.

across the world and build relationships to be etched into the fabric of our lives for ever. Not just a shift in the sands of time, but a kaleidoscope of so many changes. Little did we know this was to be the start of a new era, a new industry and a new life.

This was never going to be just a move across town: there was a real feeling of anticipation, something in the air, a buzz of excitement and a hint of things to come. All we had was a dilapidated building with two guys knocking down walls, putting new walls up and working to a plan that at its best would be guesswork. But what was happening was different from anything we had done previously. It was something new, new to the town of Bolton and new to the whole of the country.

We now had to contend with an area of eleven thousand square feet where most gyms in the country occupied a space of between five and six hundred square feet and provided just one thing, weight-training.

When starting out, the only thing we had in mind was weight-training and a sauna. We then decided to make this basic product better by laying carpets, chroming the equipment and adding some foliage. This would elevate the product, but in truth they were just the same weights. The challenge was all around us. The empty spaces needed to be filled and at this early stage we really did not know what to do. We did know success would happen, but what else was there? We could already feel the response. People were making enquiries,

Gym equipment made by the local Blacksmith in 1972 – before the mass market of the equipment of today.

popping their heads round the door to ask questions. We had more enquiries in a week than a whole year in Bank Street.

Bill and I had borrowed money to pay off our mortgages. We put our houses up as collateral to secure a £7,000 loan from the bank. This was negotiated by our accountants Barlow Andrews. We were probably spending in total about £10,000 to build a luxury health club, well it was only 1971!

The start of this enterprise was about three things: a gym, sauna, showers and very little else. Only a meagre part of the population wanting some organised fitness and we were not yet sure if it would prove popular with the ladies. There were no statistics or research to look at so we could only make a guess as to what people would want.

The workforce of Bolton revolved around engineering, the remnants of the fast diminishing textile trade and mining. It was also a time of the three-day week introduced by the Conservative government to conserve electricity which was severely limited due to the industrial action taken by the miners. We also had huge rises in inflation. These were major issues: energy, coal, electricity, gas, strikes galore, certainly not the best time to start up a new business. It seemed fitting that we would open three days for men and three days for women. How we would have coped today with human rights and equality I do not know.

From a One Man Band to employing a team of fifteen.

By now, you are probably getting the picture about how things keep repeating themselves. To introduce lifestyle change was, at the very least brave, and at its best crazy; calculation and logic it was not!

Whilst all of this was going on, we were building and preparing for the opening. People would pop in to satisfy their curiosity. I can clearly remember in November 1971 standing on a pile of bricks in the proposed reception area to give prospective clients a tour and tell them what we were going to do. The tour consisted of no more than going from room to room of half finished alterations trying to explain what a gym or health club was. In today's world everyone has some idea of what a club looks like. I did this tour perhaps ten times a day with every day being pretty much the same until one day something happened that lifted our spirits and foretold our future.

It was just another day, another pile of bricks and another customer satisfying his curiosity. This time however, the accent was American.

'Who's in charge here?' a voice asked. Those words came from the mouth of John Rodewig, European Vice-President of Eaton Transmission. An American global company with a site just a few miles down the road in Walkden. After introducing myself, I offered to give him a tour of the not yet finished Bolton Health Studio.

Bill's wife Kath (on the right) would help us to launch the Nut Tree Restaurant.

John was not alone: behind him in typical American fashion followed an entourage of six assistants, fellow directors or managers, all being dragged along in his slipstream.

'What are you going to do there?'

'What kind of equipment will there be?'

'Where are the changing rooms?'

We were all being swept along by this force of energy, this American tycoon wielding his power of command with a flourish.

As we came back to what would be the reception he came to an abrupt halt. He asked, 'What will it cost and can we do a deal?'

It was at this time the deal was made and we signed up our first corporate membership of twenty-seven people from the company of Eaton Transmission. Not a bad day's work for a couple of lads fresh from a building site!

I still believe to this day that John Rodewig could see beyond the pile of bricks, mortar, dust and unfinished work. He had the vision to see that the rolls of carpet and chromed equipment would be the making of a Health Club with some sophistication. The decoration and addition of exotic plants throughout the building followed, and with it something that helped define the future.

The Christmas chart topper in 1971 was Benny Hill's 'Ernie the Fastest Milkman in the West.' The weather was sunny, but cool. We

1980's – when equipment became King.

would welcome in a New Year that introduced decimal currency. East Pakistan was replaced by Bangladesh and there was much celebrating at the opening of Disney World in Florida. T Rex had a run of ten weeks at No 1 with hits of 'Hot Love' and 'Get It On.'

Christmas for me, Bill and our families was celebrated like most others. There was however a tension that we were entering a new decade of some uncertainty. This was a time when you could by a house for about £1,000. A dozen eggs for 23p. A trip to the cinema would cost 30p and filling up your petrol tank would set you back just 7p a litre.

The Christmas period saw us putting the finishing touches to the club: the former kitchens for the annexe to the grammar school became our shower area and locker room. The science lab was now our café bar and in due course became a full blown restaurant. The two main classrooms housed a multitude of chromium plated barbells and dumbbells with the focal point a glittering six station multi-gym of selectorised weights. No messy discs, just a pin. A standard fixture with the resistance machines of today, but back in 1971 a revolutionary concept.

Spa Bath 20 years ahead of its time before becoming part of the gym culture.

The new Bolton Health Studio opened its doors to the public on Monday 3rd January 1972. The club occupied the ground floor which measured 2225sq feet.

We had been twenty five years ahead of the game in Bank Street and the Fitness Industry was still a hobby. The launching of our new look was something of a revolution.

Within the first two years of opening, we renovated and transformed the basement to include a larger changing room with a new and bigger sauna, a spa bath and new shower area. On this occasion we spent more than three times the initial investment.

Our next decision was to move upstairs to the first floor where we built the first of our two squash courts, adding yet another facility to our portfolio of services. We now had three quarters of the building put to use.

Aerobics was still ten years away: We introduced Movement to Music that later would be incorporated to Jazz-a-Size and then Aerobics. Still ahead of the times and long before the introduction of resistance machines, we came up with a brand new concept specially designed for our members.

The first resistance machines to make their debut were in the USA when a guy called Arthur Jones launched a concept called 'Nautilus'.

Bolton Health Studio Ladies Squash Team.

These single station machines would change a whole industry. In fact, it could be said they created an industry in making weight-training safe and available to the masses. Arthur Jones was a revolutionary and appears to have been overlooked in the modern day fitness industry.

What had started out as just a gym had now become a multi-purpose all embracing health club. I believe we were the first to embrace bodybuilding alongside keep fit, aerobics, squash and spas. We had an abundance of white and blue collar workers, out of offices working out together: factory workers, bricklayers, postmen, market traders and housewives. We were a club for all people and all seasons.

We now had a full service restaurant called 'The Nut Tree' with a separate entrance for the general public. This alongside our other services was something of a model for the future and we were still only in the mid to late seventies.

Our reputation spread way beyond the boundaries of Bolton and our connections with NABBA would be the catalyst for our Training Courses.

The reputation and knowledge of physical culture expert Oscar Heidenstam, President of NABBA, was the first stop for any television people wanting information on body matters. Oscar always recommended them to go and see Ken at Bolton Health Studio.

3 Champs – Bill Pearl (Mr Universe) Bert Loveday (Mr Britain) Tony Ekubia (British Commonwealth Light Welterweight Boxing Champion).

The Man Alive Programme, fronted by Harold Williamson, was just one of the people to seek our advice for a programme they were making about changing the shape of our bodies.

I was invited to appear on BBC National Television and took along club members Bridget Gibbons, Gordon Pasquill and instructress Karen Gilmore to demonstrate various body exercises. This was followed by dozens of other invitations that elevated our status nationally. It was a long way from the school rooms, cellars gyms and the gym above the Co-op in Bolton.

The building of our Squash Courts would trigger a meeting with squash legend Jonah Barrington who happened to be playing an exhibition game at the Warrington Squash Club.

I had been asked by Tony Carter, who had become a member of our club after just returning from Australia, if I fancied going along to Warrington with him to watch the game and I was delighted to accept his invitation. I can't say I remember too much about the game or who Jonah was playing, but I do remember going into the locker room and introducing myself.

One of Jonah's first questions was, 'Do you play squash?'

'Yes!'

I then told him about the gym and also a little about us.

1980 – Bolton Health Studio team of runners ready for the World Veterans' Championship in Glasgow. Everyone of them over 40 and some in their 70's.

71

Jonah could not believe we had squash and weights all under one roof and this immediately grabbed his attention.

Where There's a Will

When I met Jonah we had already installed our first squash court: I knew instantly that this sport and particularly this man would ignite the public's appetite for the game and with the help of Tony Carter we would find a way of making squash an integral part of our club. In doing this we had once again to think differently from anyone else in the country.

With the design of our building and everywhere being wood we would not be able to build the standard brick built court.

Tony said, 'I know of a company making Portable Squash Courts that have been designed specifically to be moved around when putting on exhibition matches.' And after doing some research, Tony located one in Liverpool. Arrangements were made for him to take Bill and me to have a look at it.

In reality this was a giant folding wooden box designed as a squash court and exactly what we wanted.

The court was erected on the first floor where there had previously been two classrooms: A wooden box isolated in the middle of a room

Members in-house competition winner taking delivery of her car.

72

with struts holding it in place and a makeshift viewing gallery built on the end. It looked like a real squash court, the only difference being the sound of the ball making a thumping noise when hitting the walls.

Jonah Barrington was the greatest player ever to come out of the British Isles: six times World Champion and a man who made the game of squash the people's game.

He came to Bolton to play on our court bringing along the legendary Jahangir Khan, arguably the greatest player ever, and from New Zealand Bruce Brownlee, another world class player, all treading the boards of our court: a true ugly duckling story.

Within months we had ripped out the original court and somehow juggled the dimensions to install a second court.

Someone later did a calculation telling us 30,000 games had been played on those makeshift courts with some of the world's greatest players gracing the boards. Soon after the second installation we would have two men's and two ladies' teams competing in the Northern Counties Squash Leagues.

All of this from a Black Iron back street gym crystallising into one of the best Health Clubs in the country.

Fitness and Fatigues

The blockbuster film 'Saturday Night Fever' catapulted the names of John Travolta and Olivia Newton John to stardom and a place in cinematic history. The studios of New York would see a new craze for dance and spark a phenomenon that had little to do with either actor, but would cause a catalytic change in the world of fashion and see the birth of an industry.

Fitness, dance and fashion all came together in the late seventies and early eighties: we had shell suits, leg warmers, wrist and head bands and the casual shoe trainers which would not only change fashion but be the blast-off for a brand new exercise to music called Aerobics. This unprecedented wave of frenzy changed the world.

Casual was in, smart was out. Nike, Adidas and Reebok saturated the markets and, traditions of the past. Double-breasted suits, waist-coats and polished shoes would now be worn by the minority.

Our classes of two or three per day rose to fifty a week with names like Jazz-a-size, Funky and Tums and Bums. Jane Fonda simply called hers 'Workout.' In reality it all came under the same banner of Aerobics, but the women were always asking for more.

Ninety-nine per cent of the men didn't buy into the idea and even today it is the same: they could not go along with the finger-clicking, bottom lip-biting, rhythmic swinging of the hips, or wear the flower power headbnds, wrist bands and leg warmers.

Recognising this we looked for something the lads could do: this would come from yet another cinematic blockbuster hit 'Rocky.'

The film when released in the late seventies was a sensation and launched Sylvester Stallone to stardom. The rags to riches story with the music of Bill Curtis was, and still is, one of the most inspiring stories to come out of Hollywood: the authenticity of the training scenes and the basic simple sit-ups, pull-ups and pushing exercises all contained within the gym to a background of the motivating music of Eye of the Tiger struck me as being the ideal answer in creating a class for the men. No rhythm needed to be in time with the music, solid stuff and yes, a man thing, exactly what was wanted to motivate the men into attending the classes.

Our first attempt was to use existing music with a similar beat. I had asked Bill, Ray Berry and some of our Aerobic Instructors to come up with ideas and finally the simple name of 'Fitness' was decided.

The Fitness class consisted of around thirty basic exercises that successfully attracted men into the group classes and proved so popular we had it put onto tape and sold it to our members for home use.

With its growing popularity we went on to have our own music produced for a further tape that we called 'Fatigues.'

When the Going Gets Tough

Both these cassettes would become synonymous with our club and prove immensely popular with the lady members so we dovetailed them into our Aerobic programme.

Popular music, eight beats to the bar, rhythm and lyrics all play their part in delivering a class of exercise to music. The leader of the group should also have a good rapport with the class. Personality is probably more important than technical skills. Let's face it these people in the class are here to enjoy their exercise, so the dialogue and dynamics define the quality of the session.

Something had kept niggling at the back of my mind that had something to do with my old Sergeant Major doing drills on the parade ground, all to the sound of a brass band. Stirring music and the drill sergeant barking out left, left, left. Then with some hilarious remark about old women, pansies or some idiotic remark about your manhood, two left feet or your complete failure to be a soldier. Very often this was so funny it had the opposite effect by breaking your stride while trying to cope with the laughter. All this was about connecting with the group and developing to a sense of one. All this was going through my mind when I thought of replacing the lyrics with a dialogue of our own.

The sound bites delivered at crucial times of the exercise programme would be lines like 'When the going get's tough only the Tough get going.' Or 'If you try you might, if you don't you won't.' or 'We are beating the battle of the bulge with Fatigues.' All said tongue in cheek. All trying to capture the mood of the sergeant major and all meant to get that laugh. Fortunately or not, depending on how you looked at it, it had the opposite effect. The dialogue motivated them.

Fatigues would serve its purpose for years. Music of the top ten would come and go but the fitness and fatigues classes would go on and on and even today, a quarter of a century after we evolved the classes, people still tell me that they are still using the tape.

The boom in aerobics of the seventies and eighties has now settled. The ever demanding public are still looking for the new craze, but really there is nothing new, only variation on a theme we went through.

Fatigues Booklet and Fitness Tape.

This was a great time for us and the start of a business that attracted quality people. It would be a few years into the future when Lorraine Carey wrote of her feeling for the club and this is what she had to say:

22nd May 2013

I was shopping in Bolton one Saturday afternoon in 1991 when I saw a building with signs for Bolton Health Studio: not being from Bolton I wasn't aware of the club, but as an aspiring aerobics instructor I had to go inside...I have never looked back.

The staff were great, the club was the largest facility I had ever seen (how times have changed) and it had everything to offer so I signed up there and then. I knew immediately that I wanted to work in the club and although I was studying to become an aerobics instructor I was working as a machinist in a sewing factory, but I was determined I would work in this amazing place.

Ken, Brenda, their daughter Karen and Bill seemed ever present in the club and I made a point of engaging with them whenever I could. When a vacancy arose for a gym instructor I applied and despite having no experience I was invited in for an interview... my first application didn't go to plan I was pipped at the post by an extremely fit ex navy marine called Simon Buggy (I have since forgiven him.) However, my change came a few months later and I never regretted it.

At the Commit to Get Fit Launch when Chairman of the FIA with Seb Coe.

Bolton Health Studio trained and qualified me as a gym instructor, step and circuit instructor, body pump (one of the first clubs to teach this in the country) the list is endless. Ken and Karen saw potential in me and then asked me to move into sales in which it seemed I was a natural and had great success. I moved through the ranks of duty manager/club manager and when Karen and her husband Ian took over I expanded to area manager.

7 years later when I decided to spread my wings I wasn't sure where I wanted to be: I loved the industry and working for Ken and Karen, but I wanted to see other things. I went to register with Kelly Services Recruitment to discuss potential roles and I was offered an interview to work for them and this is how my career path changed. I then went on to manage a city centre branch and have since worked as a regional manager for both recruitment agencies and in banking.

I truly believe the encouragement, training, belief, love of the club and the team, set me up in my career. I have met so many lifelong friends and we all still speak fondly of our Bolton Health Studio days.

The pride we took in training our people was not just in the physical sense, but on how they conducted themselves in the business of health and fitness: we knew we were not going to attract people

Brenda and Ken with friends Bill and Judy Pearl and daughter Karen.

with top academic qualifications or a university degree, so we had to teach them the life and functional skills of managing people and how to fit into an organisation. Lorraine went from working on a sewing machine to being a top manager in two national companies – a great example of good training principles.

The following is yet another endorsement of how attitudes and training, with the right philosophy changed people and their lives. This is what Eileen Thomasson had to say:

Professional chemistry, that's what you could have called it when Ken and I met back in 1988. Reminiscing lately, Ken laughed and shook his head, debating I sold him the idea to uproot me from Glasgow to Bolton to manage his health club sales, but I'm not sure who was doing the selling! Either way, I have Ken to thank for my move to Bolton, as it proved auspicious, especially when I met my husband Lee, courtesy of Bolton Health Studio's parachute jumping trip – Ken claims he's entitled to a finder's fee.

Ken, Brenda, Bill and Kath welcomed and embraced me into their families like a foster child. I was kindly invited into their family hub, providing a happy and safe base outside the working environment. To this day, I still see them as my extended family.

Some memories may fade with time, but Bolton Health Studio was very special to me. I stood outside the old building the other day, looking up at the boarded-up windows, locked double-doors and crumbling paint, but all I could think about was the first time I walked through those doors....gym instructors, Becky and Paula were stood smiling happily, handing our information packs at reception – what a warm welcome.

I soon discovered that same friendly caring attitude filtered through all the staff at Bolton Health Studio. Ken had created a health club with SOUL and I was very honoured to be part of it. Members and staff alike formed positive relationships, both in and out of the club, mirroring one big happy family. Ken's ethos was underpinned by vision and passion: his leadership style was motivating and exciting, spearheading the rest of us on his never-ending journey to excel professionally and personally.

I am grateful for the day I met you Ken Heathcote, you have been a rock, an inspiration and a dear friend and I wish you well in your quest as an author.

My Dad Joe with member Bridget Gibbons.

With my wife Brenda after receiving my first Lifetime Achievement Award in 1997 and staff members Sharon Evans and Lorraine Carey.

MOMENTS OF MAGIC – THE SOCIAL CALENDAR

LA SANTA IS a sports village on the island of Lanzarote. This small sub tropical volcanic paradise is equipped with gymnasiums, swimming pools, spa and a wellness centre. It caters for all sports from racing events, badminton, diving, soccer, cycling, table tennis and much more. World class athletes are attracted to this superb venue in the Atlantic Ocean that is part of a group of islands called the Canaries.

This island in the sun has over the years attracted millions of people for holidays and in the case of La Santa a week or two for sporting activities. Bolton Health Studio supported the village with organised trips for our members by taking thirty or forty members at a time. This was just one of the many places we would go to as part of our social calendar. It was a scene that was ultimately in place for us to go that extra mile for our customers.

The social side of the business would in time become part of our culture. Another important function was that it encouraged and developed customer loyalty, even playing a part over the years in the recruitment of members.

We would organise ski trips to France and Aviemore. There were trips to the States: California, Arizona, Nevada, Grand Canyon, Vegas and Tombstone with Boot Hill full of Chinese and not American gunslingers. We also had Disco's, Charity Balls, trips to Ascot, Boxing at G-Mex, Car rallies, Squash tournaments, Award evenings, Educational conferences for staff in San Diego and San Francisco. All jollies for our customers and staff and part of our Reward and Recognition programme. It was all good fun, but equally with a certain method behind the madness.

The serious side of this extravaganza was due to surveys and studying the habits of our customers and their comfort zones. Squash players would socialise with squash players. Keep fitters with keep fitters and bodybuilders with bodybuilders. Health clubs, in fact all clubs, are very often criticised for being cliquish, with people gravitating to what is comfortable.

We noticed that at every visit people always changed in the same area in the locker room. They would go to the same piece of equipment in the gym and line up in an aerobic or circuit class in the same part of the room on each visit.

The social calendar was there to create a different mix and help pull people together who normally only socialised with their friends or colleagues. I will let Sharon Evans explain.

1st June 2013

I worked at Bolton Health Studio for 10 years, working long hours, but I can honestly say when I look back all I do is smile and think to myself that it was the best and most important time of my life.

I have friends who I have been close to now for over 25 years and they all came from there. You see it was not like going to work; it was like seeing friends every day. The health club was not just a club it was like a family whether you were staff or a member. We did things together and we knew each other inside out.

The club was a social club, not just a gym. I used to organise a lot of our social activity. We took staff and members on trips to Ascot for Ladies Day. We organised trips to Club La Santa in Lanzarote, where 30 members and staff would go for a weeks training or a weeks partying!!! We did that a least twice a year: when we got home we used to have reunion nights – any excuse for a party.

I organised Charity Balls where our members and staff had the chance to dress up and raise money for good causes. We would hire a room at the Reebok with the staff getting the local shops to donate prizes and we would sell raffle tickets and raise loads of money. Selling the tickets for the balls was never hard as we loved doing things together. I used to take photos and after each event I would make a collage and hang them in the gym. Members and staff alike loved them.

I was lucky enough to go to America twice: this was funded by Ken and Bill. I went to San Diego and San Francisco as a reward for all the hard work we put in. They were not all fun trips: we went to learn what was new in the gym world and to learn new techniques, but we also had fun.

We had member nights where we went to the local nightclub and we had one level of the club that was just for our VIP members and it was always filled with members of all ages. We were a big family and I can honestly say I had the best time of my life working there. Last year one of our members organised a reunion party

for staff and members: it was great ad we cannot wait for the next one. One of the best things to come out of it was that some of us had not seen each other for years, yet when we got together it felt like yesterday and for me that says it all. Real family and friends do not have to see each other every day or every week to know how much it means.

There will never be another place like Bolton Health Studio. I was blessed to have been a part of it and if you ask me would I change anything the answer would be a big NO!

Ladies day at Ascot.

RUNNING MARATHONS AND MARATHON RUNNERS

THERE IS SOMETHING compelling about the distance of twenty-six miles three hundred and sixty-five yards: the world seems hell bent on running marathons with over eighty different countries staging and organising events for thousands and thousands of people – people of all ages who illogically and with great determination run themselves into the ground and sometimes beyond.

This fascination for the long run is not restricted to age, gender or any standard quality or qualification: all that is asked is that you send the money, sign the waver and turn up on the day. What you do have to be prepared for is to be pulled, pushed, shuffled, herded, positioned, categorised and numbered into a well-ordered and obedient mass. All of this is then described as challenging, liberating, life-changing and fun and what is more, we love it.

This extraordinary phenomenon of modern times invites all: Dougie Tobutt, a local of Bolton and a friend of mine has run and negotiated over one hundred and twenty of these and if that is not enough he has spread those over fifty countries. Over the years he has not been easy on himself, having overcome asthma, chronic hip pain and defying the doctors, surgeons and well-meaning advice. He changed his lifestyle and diet and embarked on a regime of therapeutic exercise that gave him a pain-free life that relatively speaking allowed him to continue with this mad adventure of marathons across the globe.

In total contrast to Dougie we also have a local (well really Cheshire) lad by the name of Ron Hill. He is a double Olympian with a time of 2.0.9 to his credit and he was the first Brit to win the Boston Marathon, the most prestigious race in the world. He became not a legend in running folklore, but 'the legend.'

Ron is a Commonwealth Gold Medallist in the marathon. He is the runner of all runners having not missed a day in fifty years.

At 74 he is miraculously still running and competing, and prior to writing this, he came twenty-third in an entry of one hundred and fifty and in doing so scaled a one thousand feet peak on a five mile race.

The last marathon I competed in was the first London Marathon and probably the start of the fascination: in 1980 the top woman then and first home in a time of 2.28 was Joyce Smith. It is still a fantastic time for women's running. At this time she was over thirty-five years of age making it even more remarkable.

My time in that race and a result of her pace was 2.31.50. I tried to stay with her over the final six miles but she took four minutes out of me over the final push.

*In the presence of greatness – Ron Hill is not a legend – he is **the** legend. Note: no number.*

At forty-five years of age I came to the conclusion that what little pace I had was now receding into oblivion. Twenty-six marathons in a little over five years had exhausted my limited talent and was the closure to a memorable chapter in my life.

My venture into ultra-distance was again rewarding with forty, fifty and over a hundred miles at a time. My best run over twenty-four hours was one hundred and twenty-six miles: but it will always be the marathon I remember as the best.

The twenty-six marathons got me around a bit, but not as much as

Helping Bolton United Harriers win the 25km World team championship in 1979. Mike Freary was the winner with yours truly in 15th place and Tommy Parr 24th.

Dougie. I ran in Berlin, Boston and Bruges and also Glasgow, where I ran another time of 2.31. They were all rewarding and when you give your all for the sake of a 'time' I guess this is why people put themselves though the ordeal. Whilst Dougie went for more, I and others went for better, but whatever the outcome, fulfilment and satisfaction are the true reward.

Marathon running is just another aspect of life bringing with it a host of benefits, not the least being the people we meet. Roger Bourbon is a character of rare distinction: his run of 3.06 in 1981 was all the more remarkable because he ran the marathon in his work uniform. He was a waiter, or to be more precise a Maître De and to be even more precise a Maître De in his own restaurant on Rodeo Drive in Beverley Hills. Not only did he run a very respectable race dressed as a waiter, but he did it carrying a tray with a bottle of Champagne and a glass. Roger epitomised Hollywood: he was fun; he was a gentleman and for all these years has remained a friend. This is just one reward of being a marathon runner.

This is the start of the 24 hour race in Doncaster in 1978 with Tommy Parr manning the drinks station. I covered 126 miles and came second.

In 1982 he had a second crack at the London Marathon: still dressed in his uniform and carrying the tray he completed the run in less than 3 hours with a time of 2.47 – the fastest running waiter in the world!

He then came north to Bolton: staying with us, training and socialising with our family and club members. This was consistent with his personality and talent for being different. He was a hit with everyone he met and also a little crazy – when dining out with us he would order a Crème Caramel as a starter! Roger was good to train with, enjoyable company and crazy enough to be liked by all.

In return for our hospitality we were welcome at any time to enjoy the razzmatazz, the glitter and glitz of Tinseltown.

Two years later Brenda and I accepted the invitation and had a roller coaster week of fun and work: I even managed to do a 10k race that lived up to the hype of Hollywood. Before that however, we dined with the stars and personally met a world champion boxer and even refused an invite to a genuine Hollywood party.

8797 Sunset Boulevard in West Hollywood was the address of the world famous Spargo's, a restaurant owned and run by the equally world famous Wolfgang Puck.

He was and still is host to the famous: then it was Reagan and

Members of Bolton Health Studio en route to Berlin for the World Vets Championship in 1974.

Thatcher, the stars of Dallas, the Beverly Hillbillies, Jack Lemmon, Tony Curtis, Donald Sutherland, Karen Black and many more.

Roger's invitation would treat us to all this with the proprietor Wolfgang sitting and dining with us, compliments of our friend and owner of Romeo & Juliet's on Rodeo Drive. Champagne on tap, limo's galore in the car park and a table the envy of all. What a guy.

The razzamatazz was good, but nothing could live up to the 10k race in Century City.

'Fancy doing it?'

'You bet!'

We set off at 5am with five thousand runners turning up to register for the 6am start. It was pure show biz; band stands with live music blaring out – Hawaii five-O – The theme from Dallas – the Big Country – stalls selling everything from frozen Yoghurt to energy drinks – weighted running vests – running dumbbells – and every conceivable form of running apparel. The circus had arrived in town, but instead of animals, gymnasts and clowns we had weirdo's of every description, making the Running Waiter look quite normal.

Roger Bourbon (the greatest running waiter in the world) ahead of three of the greatest marathon runners. Just look at the expression on Rod Dixon's face (centre runner) Where did this fellow come from?

The downtown Century City skyscraper resembled a Hollywood film set, depicting a scene of the city being invaded by aliens, and the race looking like a western stampede. From the starting gun going off, the race was superbly organised. Roger finished a little ahead of me and went through one of the twelve organised taped off funnels ready prepared for the mass finish. He met me with an armful of goodies and with a huge smile on his face, the genial, exuberant, extrovert Swiss American said

'Now you know why I love America!'

The first fifty over the line were gifted with an envelope: a special invitation to the Hollywood Premier 'Return of the Jedi' at a luxury downtown cinema. Unfortunately, this was for the week after our departure back home.

Still a place in the top fifty, an armful of goodies and an experience never to be forgotten – only in America!

It would be easy to forget why we made the trip. Our business was still trying to come to terms with the boom in aerobics. Jane Fonda had jumped onto the bandwagon setting up studios to cope with demand. Central to her operation was Beverly Hills. This was the real reason Brenda and I had flown across to the States. As much as we were enjoying the 'jolly' we also needed to see what the world was

Arriving in LA and being greeted by Roger Bourbon.

seeing at the hub of the aerobic scene and to say we were disappointed was putting it mildly.

The aerobic scene in the States was in reality, far behind us in Bolton. Four thousand miles away, it was about providing safe, effective exercise. Here in the midst of the hype of Hollywood, it was fashion. Out of work dancers, young, flexible and fit enough to do two hours non stop. Delivering the class with their backs to the group was about violating everything we stood for: another lesson in life on what not to do! With forty to fifty people in each class, all female, apart from me, this was at best satisfying the fashion conscious folks of Hollywood, but not the vulnerable backs of the lasses in Lancashire. The amazingly high profile Janie made a 'Movie' called 'Aerobics' – good to look at and best left at that!

Going for my workout at the Jane Fonda Workout Studio in Beverley Hills, California.

The final night of our flying visit to the American dream was spent with our host. Coming out of Romeo and Juliet's with Roger we were greeted with a pure white stretch limo pulling up at the kerbside. Stepping out of the car in a pure white suit was a giant of a man with pure white teeth, all the more obvious with his dark complexion. Also stepping out of the car were two platinum blondes in pure white dresses.

Roger signalled for us to greet the man who stood six feet eight inches tall and looked to weigh about two hundred and sixty pounds. He was wearing a jacket you could have draped over a battleship.

'Ken I would like you to meet a friend of mine – Ken, this is Ken Norton the World Heavyweight Champion.'

This was just a daily occurrence in Beverley Hills and gifted to me because I ran marathons.

We flew back home to Bolton and reality: in tandem with running our business, I would continue to train and to train others. The real world! Our club was probably at its best throughout the eighties – not as flash or even as high profile as Rodeo Drive, but we still had the pulling power for top athletes.

In 1982 Steve Kenyon had won the three AAAs marathon in a time of 2.11.40 putting him right up there with the best. The winner of the Rotterdam Marathon, Deeks Castella, was also on top form and later that year would win gold in Brisbane with a time of 2.09. Deeks was touring Great Britain running mainly cross country 10k's but had come to Bolton for a race at a local park.

Deeks was in need of some relaxation so Steve had brought him down to our club to relax in the spa bath: having two world class elite runners use our club and chew the fat with members interested in running was both a privilege and a thrill.

At forty-five years of age there was no way I should be running with guys of their class, but when the invitation came the following morning to join them on a training run I spontaneously said 'OK;' – thinking 'Bloody hell!'

It was Steve's call: Deeks and I would take the route set out by the local runner. We took the hilly paths over road and country – skirting Winter Hill, Scout Road and the Smithills area. Thirteen miles of a gentle run for both of them: eyes-balls out affair for me. Fantastic! I hung in for all of the thirteen miles, only once losing the pace on the long incline of a hill called Smithills Dean Road. For them a regular daily run – for me – a training session of a lifetime.

At the time I was training at my peak, running 140 miles per week with quality work on two days plus racing. The quality work would include 4 x 100 – 4 x 200 – 4 x 400 metres and 4 x 1 mile intervals with fartlek (running, jogging, sprinting) – 140 miles per week for 16 weeks prior to the marathon. I would probably not have stayed the pace with Steve and Deeks had I done less training.

The marathon runners of today will have a similar programme: Ron Hill advocates this in his books 'The Long Hard Road' Part 1 and 2 – books that are now selling for £100 a time on e-bay.

Motivation

Motivation can come from anyone, at any time or in any place: just having people around can inspire and encourage us to get a little more out of ourselves. To be a coach and a competitor at the same time was a rare experience – to be involved with people coming to us who were gifted with a talent said a lot for our business.

Running – Squash – Soccer – Bodybuilders – Showbiz – and people who just wanted to run marathons brought yet again a richness to our lives.

I have been chased by a pack of wild dogs in Africa, lost my way in the

Outside Romeo & Juliet's Restaurant on Rodeo Drive.

mountains of Spain, raced the distance in snow, ice, rain and heat waves, been held up at gun point in Oregon and even met up with the notorious Krays and all because I ran marathons.

Forget your downtown Beverley Hills – what about downtown Bolton? This was a truly great time for our club. It was the start of not just the marathon boom, but the early signs of a boom in health clubs.

The tough times of Bank Street were now receding: our adventurous spirit and diverse facilities would make a statement and ask the question – 'Is this the new frontier – the model of the future?' In addition to squash, aerobics, weights and bodybuilding we now had running.

Taking it easy with Bill Pearl on his ranch in Oregon in 1979 after completing the Boston Marathon.

Still not yet fifty I would be dubbed the 'Father of the Fitness Industry,' something I remember not liking at the time, but the label stuck and our reputation grew.

YOU TOO CAN HAVE A BODY

YOU TOO CAN have a body like mine! Charles Atlas started selling his Bodybuilding Courses in the late twenties and would continue to sell the dream for three decades. During this time they were selling at the rate of seven hundred a week.

He transformed seven stone weaklings into husky he-men. His comic book pencil line drawings were one of the most powerful ads of the twentieth century; all based on young men who wished to be bigger, stronger, and more attractive and could win over the girls after having knocked seven bells out of the bully!

Angelo Sicilano, the son of an Italian immigrant who changed his name to Charles Atlas, delivered this amazing transformation by a method called 'Dynamic Tension,' a concept that pitted one muscle against the other. Millions of men huffed, puffed and blew in their bedrooms in an attempt to emulate the comic strip character who turned the tide and instead of having sand kicked in his face beat the bully to become the hero of the day.

Sixty years later, a friend and colleague Ewan Kelly would tell me he had signed up for the course in his teens. Ewan would later become a

The Charles Atlas Ad (courtesy of Bill Pearl Enterprises).

weight trainer: he is now in his mid seventies but even today he will still do the push-ups and the weights – so dynamic tension worked for him.

In reality Angelo Sicilano trained and pumped iron at the downtown YMCA in New York. His agent and marketing genius Charles Romano was the brains behind this huge and phenomenal successful campaign. In clips of four pictures and a blurb claiming to see results in just seven days Romano and Atlas captured, mesmerised and sold the dream to the world. Charles Atlas's place in bodybuilding history was coming to an end with the power of these ads losing their impact when weight-training became the thing to do in the late forties.

Muscle Beach at Venice in California triggered a new wave of popularity. This venue attracted some of the most Herculean physiques of all time. John Grimek, Steve Reeves, George Efferman, Clancy Ross and many more would inspire millions of young men to take up bodybuilding and as one era ended another would take its place.

The modern day health club/gymnasium was thirty or forty years away, but in Bolton we would unknowingly be part of the new wave that helped people to look and feel good.

Forty years later I looked back and saw how people had bought into a whole new world of fitness: Like it – Love it – Loath it – the human race is obsessed with how they look and feel. Working out is now a part of our society with some of it good and some not so good.

For years we helped people to get bigger – smaller – fitter – faster – stronger – quicker – or anything that stretched them to a new you. That was our livelihood. I believe we had the best product in the world to work with and in doing this we changed the lives of people for the better. I have seen people recover from heart disease, heart operations and even heart transplants, backs, hips, knees, every conceivable form of operation. We took them all on – the ridiculous to the sublime – the bizarre to the body beautiful – a roller coaster of challenges with an unwavering belief in our product.

The message to everyone who worked for us was 'You have the power, the skill and the product to change people's lives.' The students who came on our training courses received the same message.

Walter Gill was our first heart transplant patient. He went on to compete in the disabled games. Tony Griffin who suffers from cerebral palsy became the most decorated disabled athlete in history and forty years after walking into our club he was invited to take part in the 2012 Paraplegic Olympics. Even recently I was privileged to work with a young deaf man called Paul Mills who played soccer for GB at the Olympics in Korea.

We would build them up, slim them down, transform their shape and train them for every conceivable sport. At one point during the running craze we had more than twenty people over the age of forty who were clocking up times of less than three hours in the marathon. It was not just sound training but installing a sense of purpose.

Over the years we had thousands who bought into the belief they could be better. We had superstars like Des Drummond – he was one

Bridget Gibbon (Winner Miss Britain and Miss Universe Bikini 1977. She would go from having a great figure to a world class figure whilst training with us at Bolton Health Studio.

of the greatest rugby stars of his generation who played for Leigh and his country. Des was sent to us to train for a popular TV show called the Superstars – a programme that recruited top people from the top sports in the country. He was one of the most natural athletes I had ever seen, taking to the disciplines like a duck to water and going on to be unbeatable in the series. He should have easily won the world event, but was beaten only by manipulation of the rules – the evidence only being shown years after the event.

We were host to many professionals who not only came in to train, but would share their time with people of a like mind. Dave Prowse, the man behind the mask of Darth Vader in the original Star Wars, the world strongest man Geoff Capes and international stars from all sports and all walks of life. But, it was the world of the body beautiful that helped to launch us in the early days. This was initially sparked off by NABBA. We would see some of the greatest physiques grace us with their presence and not all of them were men.

Bridget Gibbon was seventeen when she initially joined our gym to keep fit. We had many young people who came to us to go into modelling or to enter beauty competitions, but it was Brenda who first noticed that Bridget had potential. With specific training she transformed a good figure into a great figure and then into a world class figure. She would enter and win dozens of competitions and go on to win the Miss Universe Bikini. Bridget was a lovely and genuine girl who now thirty years later still commands respect from all who know her and she is still in fantastic shape.

When Bridget was wowing them with her symmetrical shape and feminine curves another of our members was reaching for her vision of the perfect female physique and this is what she said:

'I always had narrow shoulders and wide hips, a typical Anglo Saxon figure and ordinary training didn't seem to work, so I started to train like the men.' That was forty years ago and the change in strategy changed not only the shape of Kathy Sohor's figure but changed her life as well.

Sitting across from me sixty year old Kathy looks every bit the glamorous grandmother that she is and remotely different than her muscular poses for competition. Blond, feminine and articulate she spoke of her nutrition programme, the two and a half hour workouts each day, a full time job and spending time with her grandchildren.

How do you get abs like that? she is sometimes asked.

'It is just simple training over the last forty years. To look cut and ripped is nothing more than hard training and a solid basic diet – I have now accepted people will relate it to drugs, but they are wrong. In the past I have tried Creatine but it just seemed to bloat me. I once tried the prescription slimming supplement Ephedrine (now banned) but in truth that didn't work either. I just eat good food, train hard and keep doing it week in week out. Consistency over time is the answer and I am always in shape.'

Kathy went on to say she has two children ages 30 and 39 and also 3 grandchildren ages 6, 9 and 10. She has been happily married to Mike for 31 years. She also enjoys a meal out with a glass of wine at the weekend, but for the rest of the week it is a disciplined and demanding hobby – a lesson for all of us.

Kath Sohor. A 60 year old grandmother with a six-pack (Photo courtesy of The Beef *magazine).*

Oscar Heidenstam the President of NABBA and also Editor of the Bodybuilding Magazine Health and Strength, an organisation I had subscribed to both as a member and competitor (ill equipped I may add in the latter) had followed our progress for years and when we made the leap into Mawdsley Street he would be the first to give us recognition. Health and Strength was the magazine of the day for bodybuilders: it was a niche market with a 20,000 circulation. This would be the vehicle that gave us the profile of the best club of its kind in the country.

I had been a judge at many Regional and National Bodybuilding Competitions and eventually I was asked to be a judge at Mr Universe in London.

Oscar's remarkable success in staging this global competition would put these young men who had trained and worked out in the black iron gyms from all over the world onto the greatest stages in the world. Venues such as the London Palladium, Scala Theatre, the New and Old Victoria Palace that were host to some of the world's most famous stars of music hall, vaudeville and an extravaganza of shows like My Fair Lady and Saturday Night at the London Palladium where audiences saw the great icons of showbiz: Shirley Bassey, Frankie Laine, Perry Como, Sinatra, Sammy Davies Jnr. and many more. Bodybuilders from Puerto Rico, Santiago to Sacramento, bathed in the limelight to packed audiences in these majestic theatres.

It was on one of these occasions in the late sixties I found myself sitting backstage prior to the show at the New Victoria Palace with Oscar. We were in mid conversation when a young twenty year old giant of a man in posing trunks stopped in front of us. Oscar looked up saying with some humour:

'So Arnie, what are you going to do next?'

'I am going to America where I am going to be a film star and make a lot of money!

'If I know you Arnie you will become the President of America!'

'No Oscar, I cannot become President, I was not born in America, but I could become Governor!'

Thirty years later this Austrian lad Arnold Schwarzenegger became a multi-millionaire demanding ten million dollars a film and he also became the Governor of California. Many years later I would discover he had his goals in place at the tender age of eleven. At that time, he was unaware of how he would find the vehicle to get him there, until he discovered bodybuilding.

From Charles Atlas to the Terminator, I too have been touched many times by many people who wanted to get a body like them.

Terminator

I met Arnold many times at the Mr Universe Competition. However, there was one occasion when we would meet up at Gold's Gym in sunny California where Bill Stevenson and I had gone to do some research. At that time it was situated on Venice Beach – the old muscle beach where it all started. He was in the gym training with the Belgian bodybuilder Pierre Vandestein, who was a class winner at the Mr Universe.

When we entered they were training together at the far end of the gym, but seeing us Arnold waved, stopped his workout and came across to speak to us.

'How are Oscar and the lads back in the UK?'

Walter O'Malley. Not quite the man who terminated the Terminator – but if it had been judged on points he would have won.

He was conversational, good natured, courteous and showed great respect. He was not always the same when in competition as he demonstrated with my mate from Warrington, Walter O'Malley.

The setting was the Mr World being held in Bruges: Walter was competing against two American adversaries, Arnold and Franco Columbo – two guys who were fresh from California with a Californian tan. Walter had come over from Warrington where the sun doesn't shine that often and was having to settle for a tan out of a bottle! Tanning lotion in the sixties had not yet reached a level of sophistication and when applied was often patchy and streaky. On seeing this Arnie guffawed and pointed at Walter's inadequate finish, psyching him out. Nothing would happen at the judging, but later and after the show the competitors had gathered at an English bar in the city centre.

Arnold should have kept his mouth shut, but he couldn't resist having another go at taking Walter down a peg.

'I couldn't let them Yanks get the better of me, so I went for him!' were Walter's words to me some years later.

Can you just picture these two muscular giants clashing in a bar in Bruges with Walter winning on points and the Austrian Oak or should I say the Terminator being terminated?

From then on Arnold would always refer to Walter as the 'Mad Irishman' – an affectionate term that still prevails today. He may very well be back. He is, but he stays away from Walter.

On opening in Mawdsley Street in 1972, bodybuilding was the thing: we had not yet defined a market, people were unsure of what they wanted, with weights in general still the forbidden fruit. For all our attempts in making the product more attractive, hard core bodybuilding was still the only game to play. However, we did change a few things: the carpeted area of the keep fit was now separated from the heavy boys, which by definition was making a statement. The equipment on the ground floor became more sophisticated and was chromium plated.

The heavy room in the cellar below still resembled the black iron gyms of the past, but we updated this by painting the weights air force blue and padded all the benches. It was still very basic, basic enough to deter the keep-fitters. A distinctive difference!

Because of my strong connections with NABBA, Oscar Heidenstam was eager to come to Bolton to see for himself what we were trying to do. I remember clearly his astonishment at how we had blended the two markets together. It was definitely a step up in the right direction that would prove to be significant in the future.

His involvement in promoting bodybuilding through the Mr Universe contest was known worldwide: although it was still a minority sport or a competitive spectacle, Oscar seized the opportunity to embrace our club as a beacon to demonstrate that there was another side to bodybuilding and that was Bolton Health Studio.

From the moment he saw our club, it was the place that would become the example: Bert Loveday is a former Mr Britain and current Mr Universe judge. He was a Boltonian and bodybuilding show organiser who would get involved and suddenly overnight we became the attraction for all the Mr Universe winners coming North who spent time working out with us at the studio.

Stuart Cosgrove. Started training with us in the 70's. He is a multi-title winner and extremely knowledgeable on diet, exercise and the misuse of steroids.

To mention just a few from overseas, we had Chris Dickerson, Frank Zane, Lance Dreher, Serge Nubret and the legendary Bill Pearl. They would all make our gym the place to train when appearing in shows in the North West. We also attracted the British guys like Paul Winter, Eddie McDonagh, Earl Maynard, Terry Phillips and Walter O'Malley. It would also be the place for female winners like Mary Scott, Linda Cheeseman and later Donna Hartley who would come onto our weight training course.

It gave us a chance to see at first hand how these athletes performed in training, how consistent and how hard they worked and what thought went into their training. Everyone was dedicated to the point of squeezing out every ounce of their potential. They all trained

Bill Pearl and Arnold Schwarzenegger in 1967. Later Arnie tried to lure Bill out of retirement but never succeeded. (Courtesy Bill Pearl Enterprises).

daily 6 days per week with most doing twenty or more sets per body part. Twenty sets on biceps, twenty sets on triceps, and twenty sets on each single body part. They were meticulous in the planning of their training, diet and nutrition for months ahead of the competitions. This was not just consistent with bodybuilders, but all athletes. The ones who wanted to make it, worked the hardest.

The opportunity of working with all these people came because we broke the mould. The multi-purpose Health Club was more than a gym and brought together under the same roof some of the greatest athletes. It was unique.

We were instrumental in bringing Bill Pearl over from the States to do a tour of seminars and sell his book 'Keys to the Inner Universe.' I had somehow managed to get Bill and Jonah Barrington together – two entirely different disciplines in every way. One was mobile, fast and variable, the other immobile, systematic with everything available in the gym to reach a peak, a contrast in training and preparation a world apart.

However, the common ground was extraordinary, with the eye for detail unbelievable. The mental and physical dedication of time, effort, and a hunger to look at every single facet of preparation was outstanding, humbling and motivational at the same time.

It was a privilege to work with these people: to talk, to share their knowledge, dedication and their idiosyncrasies.

You too can have a body like Bill Pearl, Arnold Schwarzenegger and Charles Atlas if you make the time and effort and have the right mental approach. But all things being equal you also need talent and a single mental approach, with or without the advantages of science.

That single mental approach would also apply to us as a club. Bodybuilding would not define us: a more holistic approach over the next thirty years would.

We could not escape the new ideology of bodybuilding; we had welcomed and embraced it. However, it would not be without growing pains and an even more sinister connotation that went with the art and science of developing Herculean physiques that had first started on Muscle Beach in the forties.

It was obvious the top guys at the Mr Universe Competition were taking training to a new level. It would take much more than just doing twenty plus sets to develop a top physique. Each body part would need to match – symmetry was as important as size – huge muscle mass was not enough! Two and three hours in the gym six day per week became the norm for the ambitious bodybuilders, with nutrition vital to success. It was also becoming obvious that genetic inheritance was a non-negotiable. If you didn't have the natural attributes you were not in the race.

All the training in the world, the six protein shakes each day, pasta, protein and the right plasma conversion to muscle only favoured the few. The age of innocence, dynamic tension, the purity of bodybuilding we loved and admired was about to change.

THE 40TH

TRAGEDY IS NEVER far from our lives. I was a sixteen year old apprentice working in the building industry for a company called W. Lionel Grays who had a maintenance contract with a hospital in Manchester. As all sixteen year old apprentices do, I was fetching and carrying. If my boss told me to go and fetch some water off I would trot to look for the nearest tap.

Mid morning I found myself in a hospital ward full of children who looked about nine or ten years old, all sitting on their beds or playing games around a table. None of them had any hair. Clearly I was in the wrong place.

Standing there bewildered a nurse asked me what I wanted.

Mumbling I managed to say, 'I just want some water' and with this she then guided me to a small bathroom.

'What's up with them?' I asked the nurse.

'They all have leukaemia: they are very poorly and having special treatment which will help prolong their lives but not cure them.'

Ken and Brenda taken at the start of the 40th birthday event.

She then went on to explain that only a few of these young people were expected to live beyond the age of twenty: their lives could be extended with care and treatment, but as yet, no cure had been discovered.

I still remember that sense of loss sixty years after being made aware of this terrible disease. At the time it did not hit home, it did not create any immediate sense of need. At sixteen what could I do? But the sight of those children imprinted itself on my mind forever. I suppose at that young age it is as much as we can handle in just growing up. However, my opportunity to do something for this worthy cause would occur twenty-four years later.

As our business continued to grow we discovered marketing was the definitive factor in building up that business. The mistakes made in Bank Street had taught us what not to do. The turnaround came with our promotional literature comprising of newspaper advertisements, mail shots and various events we were organising.

I was finding that going out talking to groups and working within the community was rewarding and raised our profile. We accepted approaches from various charities including the sponsorship of Guide Dogs for the Blind. We also sponsored a local school soccer team and a netball team. However, what I really wanted, was to do something we could make our own, something to excite the people.

In the back of my mind and trying to break free were memories from the past. I had to do something special, even something spectacular, something to help those children who would never see the age of twenty-one. For that I needed to look for someone who was a master at promoting his business, a business with similarities to ours and that person was Jack La Laine.

Jack lived in the San Francisco area of America: he was a front man for a chain of Health Spas throughout California. He was also a TV celebrity many years before the UK became a celebrity nation. Jack earned his celebrity status by doing amazing feats of strength on his birthday and on TV. One of these was pulling a 'Tug' across the bay of San Francisco with his hands and feet tied together. One year he swam the un-swimmable part of the bay between the mainland and Alcatraz and yes, again with his hands and feet tied together. Another of his feats was doing one thousand press-ups and one thousand chin-ups live on TV. The Press and TV coverage was great publicity for the Jack La Laine Health Spas and everyone who was into fitness in California knew of Jack. I was an avid reader of bodybuilding magazines and had followed his amazing stunts long before we opened Bolton Health Studio.

As my fortieth birthday approached my mind turned to two things: (1) the kids I had seen twenty years ago. (2) How could I help the ones of today? To do a Jack La Laine was out of the question. We did not have a 'Bay' and I was not equipped physically to do the other things. I did however have my own strengths and so I set myself a different set of disciplines.

I was not so sure where the disciplines would come from, but I knew whatever I did would have to have an early start, so a forty mile run seemed appropriate.

Running forty miles before breakfast seemed a tough start to the day! To follow with another discipline it would have to be something not as demanding on the legs. I had worked on a system of exercise called PHA, Peripheral Heart Action. This works opposing muscle groups and uses the activity in each group as a buffer to circulate the

On the steps of Bolton Town Hall before setting off on the run with Jonah and Madeline Barrington, Tommy Parr, Mike Freary, Norman Ward and Frank Morris.

oxygen to other muscle groups. The idea is for you to first exhaust a muscle group, and then work an opposing group to force fresh oxygen into the tired and exhausted muscles.

Following the run I needed to work the upper body to near exhaustion by sequence. This is when I thought of doing a circuit of exercises that would work all of the upper body areas. The Bench Press for chest, arms and shoulders. The Dead Lift would work trapezium and lower back. Pull Downs working upper back and biceps and Bent-over-rowing a different part of the back. By using this system I would be utilizing the maximum oxygen levels and resting various muscle groups in turn. I would need to do a circuit of exercises that eventually racked up to 40,000lbs and had to be completed in forty minutes maximum.

After the event with Rodney Marsh, Francis Lee and Jonah Barrington.

Squash was to be the next discipline and to make this interesting it needed known opponents and that is where the celebrities would come in: Francis Lee of Manchester City and England and a former Bolton Wanderers player was a volunteer. Franny had come to our club to see what all the fuss was about with this new craze for squash. He didn't need much persuading as he was always keen to help out with a charity event and we could not have found a better cause than Leukaemia in Children. Rodney Marsh, a team mate and former City player, also took part. Rodney and Franny were two quite distinct personalities. Rodney was quite flamboyant, always joking. Franny was more serious. Our good friend Jonah Barrington, the best player to have ever come out of the UK was also up for helping out.

This giant of World Squash should not have been gracing the courts with the likes of me, but what a great man he proved to be by being a part of this group and helping us to raise money for this noble cause.

For me to be on court with this legend and I should really say these legends was both a privilege and a reward for what I was attempting. My fourth opponent was a news reporter from a local radio station whose name I must confess I do not remember (If you are reading this, thank you for helping with the wonderful cause!)

Because this challenge had never been tried before, we had no idea how long it would take. I had allowed a little over five hours for the run with a short rest before the second discipline. Starting out at 7am from the Town Hall Square meant I would be starting on the weights at around 12.30pm. There were no hitches, everything was going to plan and on target with the time limits I had set myself. I had some great company throughout the run with Jonah and Madeline Barrington doing the first ten miles. Mike Freary, a 10,000 metre British record holder also accompanied me not forgetting a good Bolton United Harriers pal, Tommy Parr. There was a terrific atmosphere throughout the whole event with an almost carnival feeling. I don't know how confident every one was, or if anyone thought at some stage I was going to blow or drop dead! Yes, that has been said a few times, but I felt good for the duration of the event.

The weights were set up on the Town Hall Square: our son-in-law, Ian Thorpe, had manufactured a self standing pulley machine so that I could do the appropriate repetitions for the exercises of pull-downs and bench press with a pre-loaded bar.

Using each exercise, I would do ten sets of a given number of repetitions to accumulate to a total of 40,000lbs in the time duration of forty minutes. The four exercises were Pull Downs, Bench Press, Dead Lift and Bent-over-rowing.

Harold Wrigley who was a senior judge at the Mr Universe Contest and organiser of the Mr UK Contest in Manchester, volunteered to monitor and register the circuit to make sure I kept to the weights and repetitions, not that I could cheat, with a few hundred people on the square and the Bolton Evening News taking photographs and writing a report for the newspaper.

The whole thing was going exactly to plan: I had loped through the forty miles and eased my way through the lifting with hardly any real energy depreciation. There was almost a little blip when I was on the last set of the circuit. Harold had said that I needed to keep it going to meet the deadline so I increased the speed of the last set almost causing me to be sick. A warning I suppose that I was working right up to my limit and any extra effort would take me over the edge. The lifting now completed I had to play four people at squash with three of them being athletes, athletes of some quality.

Jonah graciously gave me three points, beating me 9-1 – 9-1 – 9-1. This was a bit like the local soccer team playing Real Madrid, with the local team scoring three goals. It would not happen unless Real Madrid wanted it to happen.

In the second game I went on to beat Franny, surprising him by still having some running left in my legs, though it is fair to say Franny was not a practised squash player, I am sure that he was being kind just like Jonah! Rodney, however, had sussed me out and came on court and continually used the drop shot. He had realised that what little speed I had left had been dispersed on the run. I lost to Rodney 3 games to 1. The final game with the Newscaster went my way. I won 2 and lost 2. All the games, except of course Jonah's, were meant to be competitive and test me to my limit. The only discipline remaining now was the 400 consecutive sit-ups.

Twenty minutes later I was showering and ready to watch some of the best squash players in the world – what a way to finish the day!

The Stuff of Legends

With the unprecedented squash boom in the mid 1970's reaching epidemic proportions, Jonah had become a household name. Six times world champion and a reputation for being the fittest man in the world gave him a huge presence and a certain mystique. When it came to training and technique he was without doubt second to none. He was not the most talented of players, but what he lacked in that area he made up for with his attention to detail and insatiable aptitude for fitness.

I believe he changed the face of squash: his Egyptian and Pakistani counterparts were dominating the world's squash scene, but the level of Jonah's fitness was adding a new threat to the 'craft and touch' players in the game. His left-handed precision added a new dimension. His fitness and ability to retrieve every ball made the touch players vulnerable and forced them to play him at his own game. Fitness became as much a part of the game as craft, with endurance becoming as much a part as skill.

After my fourth game Jonah played an exhibition match with our Squash Pro Tony Carter. Following this match, and to raise more money for our charity, Jonah was scheduled to play the World No.4 Hiddy Jahan.

Jonah entered the court alone with the spectators wondering why: he then said,

'I am sorry Hiddy will not be playing today as he has engaged

Brenda presenting a cheque for £3,700 to Dr Kumar Head of Paediatric Research Christie Hospital.

one of these people called an Agent but I am sure the person I will be playing against will astonish you. This young man is just 16 years old: just a few months ago I was beating him 3-0 3-0 3-0.

He has been living in a caravan in our garden in Birmingham for three months and during this time I have been coaching and training him exclusively every day.'

'Before coming to me he played the World No 1 Geoff Hunt who beat him 9-0 9-0 9-0. Later this year he will play Geoff Hunt again in the World Championships – he will lose the match 3 games to 2. Next year he will reach the final of the World Championship and win.' He then introduced Jahangir Khan onto the court. He would go on to fulfil all of Jonah's predictions by beating him and not giving him one single point. Over the next seven years Jahangir would not lose a game and in some matches not even a set.

Some thirty-seven years later, my son Paul told me that Jonah's speed and presence in those games with Tony and Jahangir on that day motivated him for months to come. That was the power of Barrington – an extraordinary player, a brilliant coach and a man who knew squash like no other.

For the people who may think this challenge an exhausting depletion of our human energies and particularly dehydration issues, I took liquid only when needed! Today there is an enormous amount of hype about drinking water: I see people drinking unnecessary amounts. It would seem they are almost fearful of not having a bottle in their hand just in case they feel the need to take in fluid.

Our bodies are designed to monitor and control our levels of fluid: our brain is designed to accommodate the balance that is needed to keep us safe. Safe without force feeding.

In fifty years of training and competing, I have only once had fluid problems and that was during a twenty-four hour run in a heat-wave. I did not suffer dehydration, I rather suffered from over-hydration through force feeding fluid into the system hoping to compensate for the weather. The result was constant retching for five hours until I recovered and then going on to finish the race. That day, over twenty-four hours, I covered 126.5 miles. The miles and the stamina were not a problem: it was the over consumption of fluid that was the problem.

The night of my fortieth birthday, I went home with the family and invited the people who had helped out on the events. We celebrated with a party for everyone who wanted to see the whole event come to its conclusion. At 4 am we toasted in the dawn with bacon butties (not forgetting the brown sauce), strawberries and champagne.

Forty miles – 40,000lbs – 4 squash matches – 400 sit-ups – champagne and strawberries. You have to get your priorities right!

We didn't get to bed until after 6am: the legs were still twitching from the efforts of the disciplines but the whole event had been a huge success. It was money well earned for a most deserving charity with lots of effort from lots of people.

Our first effort of getting involved in a charity was in 1975 and raised in excess of £3,700. We presented a cheque to Dr Kumar, Head of Paediatric Research at the Christie Hospital who would show his appreciation many times during our various campaigns.

Over the years, events have become more sophisticated through charity balls with companies and sports personalities all putting their backs behind worthy causes. Our efforts compared to the magnificent events of today were small, but someone had to start somewhere.

My fortieth birthday was just the beginning. In the years to come we would be involved with many more. It became part of our culture and in a small way formed a part of our identity.

At a later date we would link up with Doug Farnworth and the people from Turton Rotary, but that is another story.

Our squash pro Tony Carter with Jonah Barrington after playing an exhibition match.

115

ARE YOUR STAFF QUALIFIED?

MY ANSWER TO the ever present question could only be NO. At that time there wasn't anything that offered a solution for either them or us.

BAWLA (British Amateur Weightlifters Association) was the official controlling body for the sport of weightlifting. Their course taught people to do the 'Clean and Jerk' the 'Two Hands Snatch' and the 'Two Hands Barbell Press.' None of these were of any use to our customers.

Another option was the forces physical education course, but this was restricted to HM troops. So again the answer to the question was NO.

Every member of our staff had been trained by us to a high degree, but this was never going to be enough. The universities and colleges would not get their heads around this for a few years and it was probably in the late eighties before this came about. Physiotherapists were busy trying to rehabilitate the injured and spend time preventing injury; exercise physiology didn't mean a thing. There would be no other alternative than for us to invent a qualification, something desperately needed for an emerging market.

Where do you start? How do you put a training course together to train people to train others? What are the criteria? What comes first? Who delivers this? What about the specialised areas of nutrition, anatomy and physiology? Why should we be believed? We were just two guys who had opened a Health Club. Who knew what was successful? This was in the late seventies; our membership was close on two thousand. We had good retention and good feedback from our customers so we used the results as our starting point delivering what had worked for us, but what would eventually make the course successful was the authenticity.

We had good established tutors with many years of experience who practised what they preached with safe and effective instruction. They knew not only about the technique, but also how important it was to look after the customer. They had a presence in the gym and on the course – an essential ingredient in the tool kit of the instructor. In every sense of the word a good coach has authority, presence, and the right attitude, builds confidence in the client, creates rapport and practises empathy. The gym is a workplace the coach can be proud of in doing what he or she is doing. This is their domain and something that we taught to the students. Technique, safety and knowledge were important, but presence, personality and attitude were paramount in not being just a good instructor, but a great instructor. We delivered all this to our students.

Our first attempt at running a Weight Training Instructor Course was sheer guess work. We literally stood up and told people what we were doing and what we felt was right and proper. It was not so much a course, but more of a seminar. We had the Club to show what was working. Customer Service was at the top of our agenda. We had living proof of how it was working. We brought in David Fevre, a top class soccer and rugby league physiotherapist. David would go on to be the physio for Manchester United at the time they won the treble. He is probably the best physio I have ever met in my fifty years of advising and helping people on how to train people, and how to help people to overcome injuries. There would be other super physio's, but David was the best: working with us on our courses would in future years help him to build his presentation skills to great effect.

Our expert Nutritionist was Karen Thomas: a lecturer and motivator with a soft Scottish accent. Karen had great experience and a wonderful presence that fitted perfectly into our team of presenters. Bill and I, along with Ray Berry, delivered the various subjects on coaching skills, breathing techniques and something we called 'policing the gyms' which we saw as vitally important. The exact criteria at the time were yet to be developed. We literally based it on what we did with our customers and what we believed was right for the students.

In those early days Free Weights dominated the gyms and could be a real problem for keeping areas safe. Health and Safety was still far into the future. We had our own standards and criteria for policing the gym and this was an important element for our course.

To give the course some respectability we needed to have a national identity. I approached Oscar Heidenstam the President of the National Amateur Bodybuilding Association and also the Editor of the Health and Strength Magazine. Oscar was delighted and saw this as a compliment to both him and the organisation. We paid a percentage of the course fee to NABBA which helped to swell its coffers. It would also see them enrol many new members.

The challenge with putting a National Qualification onto the market was establishing standards. The few weight training books that were in circulation would describe the techniques and it was easy enough to demonstrate these to others. The important thing when we delivered the training to others was that the technique remained the same wherever we were. This meant we had to put together a framework to establish a standard for each exercise and the technique had to include every part of the movement. The breathing sequence, correct positioning of the feet, head, torso and posture. This framework would be the foundation for a basic standard across all the exercises being delivered anywhere at any time.

When delivering the courses in other parts of the country we used to spot-check them. On one occasion, we had a course on in Stroud which was not far from Heathrow and Bill Pearl who was over in the UK at this time just happened to call in to see just what we were about. Bill Stevenson was directing the course that day and Pearl made a comment saying 'You would think everyone would know how to do a Curl,' and Bill Stevenson replied 'It's not about the exercise, it's about the standard!'

Those standards would apply to every single exercise. During the first year the students were provided with just handouts. As the courses grew, we formed a Manual that was just a simple and basic booklet of 42 pages entitled The NABBA Weight Training Instructor 2 Day Weekend Course. At a later date we would expand on the basic manual to write and develop nine other courses, each with their own manual and some with a video and audio. The course would eventually embrace the concept of distance learning, yet another first for this growing industry.

The arrangement with Oscar and NABBA was a great move for both of us. Even at the time when I was running the back street gyms in the fifties I had always been a member and active supporter and enjoyed a good relationship with the association. I was made a Life Member in 1956 and the following testimonial appeared in my book 'The Gym Business.'

At last Ken Heathcote has written a book about his long and successful career as owner/director of probably one of the best known and certainly one of the longest running modern Health Studios in Bolton.

Ken Heathcote can tell you from personal experience all the many traps you may well fall into. The secret has always been, as with all manner of business; carry on where the average person would give up.

Oscar Heidenstam, President
NATIONAL AMATEUR BODYBUILDERS ASSOCIATION

The courses would continually progress and the industry would continue to grow: the level of sophistication would demand a better image and we would be forced to re-examine our profile in the market place. Whilst all of this was happening we were still churning out instructors to work in the industry.

TRAINING THE TRAINERS

MOST THINGS IN life come down to two or three things. The game of football is all about scoring goals or conceding goals. A boxer needs to hit his opponent and avoid being hit himself. In business you have to have a greater income than your expenditure and the only two sure things in life or death are taxes. These over-simplifications are not really too far from the truth.

Michael Phelps who was the world's greatest swimmer of his time said "I do nothing else but eat, sleep and swim." When Freddy Roach engineered the defeat of our lad Ricky Hatton with the fists of Mani Pacio, he said it was no accident! Thousands of right hook practices at the start of every training session would expose the flaw of Ricky's

Students on a training course.

left hand when throwing his right. Sir Alex Ferguson the greatest football manager of his time across all sports has developed a great culture for players to grow and mature whilst silently agreeing with another genius Albert Einstein's principle of not teaching his pupils, but creating the right conditions to learn.

However, there is one common denominator in the pursuit of excellence and that is that discipline prevails in everything we do. The rules of coaching are simple; it is the discipline that is hard.

I spent four decades helping people to lose weight. Eat less is the discipline – doing it is the work. Training athletes is all about defining the critical skill and constant refining is the honing of that skill. Repetition is the mother of all skills. Boring is productive. The coach knows this and the job of the coach is to deliver the skill and find ways of overcoming the boredom. There are only a small percentage of people who embrace the philosophy of training; the rest have to be

Weight Training Instructor.

coaxed, persuaded, cajoled, disciplined, manipulated and even bullied. Every great coach at some time will have used all these techniques. The coach knows this and the athlete respects it.

For most of my adult life I have been involved in training others. It started in the fifties with running that small backstreet black iron dustbowl gym in cellars, school rooms or anywhere we could find some space. Those very early days were all about learning the simple techniques and repetitively reproducing the very simple execution of skill and when starting up in business it was natural for us to train our own staff. However, the customer always wanted more! The questions we were most frequently asked were not how do I lose weight or how do I gain muscle or how do I get fit, it was always are your Instructors qualified? It could be quite intimidating for people entering a Health Club or Gym for the first time and they would rightly fear taking up an exercise programme without proper guidance. Five decades ago there was little knowledge of working out in gyms. People thought it was all about sweat, bulging muscles, men looking a little comical in leotards, weights that were a bit butch for the ladies and a fear of looking muscular. Having proper instruction was a prerequisite for the new or first step to their new lifestyle.

THE RE-BRAND

THE WEIGHT TRAINING Instructor Course would become the Fitness Instructor Course. The name would change from NABBA to Focus Training. The identity of a bodybuilding figure would change to a Key – a Key to the future – a Key to success – a Key to a new career.

Focus Training would grow to become one of the top courses in the UK. The NABBA course had at one stage been the number one course in the country for weight training. We had built a great platform, but we now had to start all over again.

For people coming into the industry it was confusing together with the people who had already pledged themselves to the old qualification. A difficult time, an exciting time and the time to come would be terrific.

Now under a new identity we went on to develop it into ten different courses each with their own manual.

The framework of delivery and the method of presentation was both efficient and exciting. These were not chalk and talk deliveries or a tick box, paper-driven knowledge-based training. It was an interactive engaging course expressing the very things valued on the job.

The very philosophy of being personal is about human interaction. It is about engagement, eye contact, body language and empathy. Being a trainer or a coach is all about getting the best out of the student and the instructor. A great example of this is reflected in how it is valued by the individual and by the recipient of the qualification – the gym owner. The following stories are just examples of how this worked for both.

Steve Kear came to us with a request to do both the Basic and Senior courses. At the time he was working in the building industry in plant hire.

The Basic course was essentially for the Gym Instructor and the more advanced Senior course leaned more towards the management side of the business. Steve went on to say he did not have a great deal of time as he was emigrating to Australia and was it possible to do both courses in a short period of time?

We did not see a problem with that provided he passed the exam for the Basic course first. If the calendar of events suited him we could fast track the process. It was agreed and Steve did both courses and passed with distinction.

It would be many years later before I saw Steve again and this time it was at a conference in Stratford upon Avon. I was just leaving the conference centre when a voice suddenly said,

'Ken, may I have a word with you?'

At first I did not recognise him as it had been five or six years since he had set off to start a new career and a new life in Perth Australia.

He said he had really tried hard to get work in the fitness industry in Australia but not quite made it until one day he walked into a club called Bull Creek Health and Fitness.

He was interviewed by a guy and informed they had three clubs but were fully staffed at all three. This guy was answerable to the General Manager, who was an Irishman and just happened to be on site at the time of the interview. Steve was asked to leave his CV and if any vacancy became available they would give him a call and off he went to another office where the GM was. It just so happened that Steve had put his NABBA Certificate on top of his CV and the GM caught a glimpse of it and asked the guy what it was.

At the expense of repeating the information I think it is worth showing the letter Steve would write for this book:

4 June 2013

Hi Ken

I remember at the eager age of 22 (1988) I attended Bolton Health Studios for my first of the NABBA courses. I recall I was nervous and didn't have any idea of what to expect, also at this point how this new direction in my life from a heavy plant mechanic to trainee fitness instructor would have such an impact on me. One thing I will always remember is how busy the club was, every area, and each floor was a hive of activity.

The classroom was typical old school style and Ken Heathcote introduced himself to all of the students and one by one he called our names. I couldn't believe he knew all of our bosses back at the clubs. I mean I was working in a health club in Eastbourne and there was I sat in Bolton listening to Ken talk about my boss like he was his neighbour. He did the same to all of us – that's what I call 'an attention getter.'

The basic 3 day course was amazing and still to this day I firmly believe the delivery of that syllabus, culture and ethos is the

foundation of a professional fitness instructor. I can hear Ray now saying 'the mirrors are the eyes in the back of your head – while you are with one client you must continually scan the gym using the mirrors offering assistance where needed.'

The first course seemed reasonably in-depth and was a good balance between theory and practical and I passed with flying colours. The Diploma was much more difficult and included a 6 week home learning pack which had to be completed before you attended the course. The syllabus became my bible; it was written in a way that made it addictive to read with really clear diagrams of the anatomy and clear explanations. I had always found it difficult to learn and absorb at school. However, I found myself really hungry for the information delivered on the NABBA courses. Once I had passed this course I then embarked onto the

Focus Training.

Advanced Diploma which was really in-depth and tested me to my full potential. Each time I came away from the health studios with my newly found knowledge I felt more empowered as a fitness instructor and desperate to use this knowledge on the gym floor.

In 1990 I travelled to Australia on a 12 month working visa, probably the best part of my life. I arrived in Perth and quickly started to look for work with the fitness industry. As you can imagine they were way ahead of the UK in the development of health and fitness clubs. I remember I was finding extreme difficulty to land a job. One day I walked into a club called Bull Creek Health and Fitness. I did the usual introduction of myself and was told by the fitness manager 'sorry no vacancies.' I asked him to copy my details and qualifications. The photocopier was in the General Managers office and as the Fitness Manager started to copy, the GM spotted the NABBA certificates and called me into the office and said 'so you know Ken Heathcote' – wow you can imagine how I felt, how amazing to have something in common with this guy I was talking to across the other side of the world and of course I talked myself into a job! The GM was originally from Ireland and had previously embarked on the NABBA courses.

To this day I still hold the values taught to me on the NABBA courses close to my heart and whenever I am in one of the clubs I take the time to speak to instructors to ensure they are holding similar values.

To summarise I believe Ken Heathcote and the development of his NABBA courses and total commitment to the Fitness Industry is responsible for ensuring Fitness Instructors became a recognised and respected profession.

Regards
Steve Kear

The GM had recognised the certificate as he had done the same courses and Steve was immediately invited into the office for a chat. He told him he had done the course in Bolton and the GM asked about the 'lads.' How was Ken, Bill and Ray etc – a small world – a little course with a big reputation and yes, Steve got a job.

The story of Steve Kear is just one of many typical stories to come out of the history of our courses. The Toronto Police was another story – six people from their drug squad were enrolled on the course and gained their qualifications. We had one pupil who on passing his Personal Trainer Course went on to teach a Sheikh in the Arab Republic.

We also had celebrities from the TV show 'The Gladiators' – James Crossley who played Hunter and Diane Youdale who played Jet. Jet went on to become the most popular of all the gladiators.

We also had success with some of the top hotel groups in the country – The Marriott, DeVere, Hilton and many others along with local authorities from Aberdeen to as far south as Eastbourne.

Diploma.

INSPIRATIONAL MARIANA

MARIANA MET HER husband Frank Miskell, a Bolton chap, when he was working in her native land of Bulgaria. When she became pregnant they decided to make the move back to the UK to settle where Frank's family lived.

New to the country she was looking to integrate into the British way of life, so when Frank's brother Peter who was a member of Bolton Health Studio told her about the club she came down to pay us a visit. By this time Mariana had given birth to a son who they named James. Mariana now had two incentives. One was to take up an exercise regime and two was to regain her figure.

Photo of Mariana.

She had been a member at the club for about a year when she started to take an interest in our training courses. She says,

'I clearly remember asking you what I had to do to become an instructor.' We had previously talked about working in the fitness industry and I remember saying we were always on the look out for good staff.

Mariana had already made many friends at the club and she was happy with the social life the studio had given her, but she could now see the possibility of not only a better social life but also the promise of a new career.

Her decision to gain some qualifications was a decision that would change her life! She took to being a trainer like a duck takes to water. Her infectious personality, an appetite for work and striking good looks would make her one of the most popular trainers we had ever produced. She would go on to do the Basic and Senior course, the Aerobic Instructor course, Nutrition course, Sports and Injuries course and finally win the Diploma.

Mariana took up employment with us and later went on to work for the David Lloyd Organisation and also for Virgin Health Clubs. She is amazingly proficient in all disciplines – aerobics – salsa – zumba – pump and many others. She is now the owner of property in Bulgaria and the UK and says work now comes to her instead of having to go out to look for it. She is already laying plans for when her teaching career come to an end with her latest venture of an online clothing company. She is not just proud of her success, but grateful for the opportunity that gave her a new life.

This is what Mariana would say about her life changing experience: 'In the first years of my life in the UK I've found a new fitness career by enrolling for Focus Training under the encouragement of Ken Heathcote.

In conversation with him I remember expressing my interest in the training and becoming a fitness/aerobic instructor. Ken said that this would be such a great opportunity for me as I would be able to teach classes in Bolton Health Studio.

I remember he said You may as well start teaching here as you are already in the club training every day. Those were the key words that made me finalise my decision, the rest is history.

I did achieve full diploma status by completing all the various fitness levels on offer, plus on-going training over the years.

It has been a truly enjoyable and yet challenging journey. After 17 years I am still teaching my classes with passion and enthusiasm. This rewarding job has given me so much more energy, inspiration, a youthful and positive outlook on life, and the opportunity to meet amazing people and make great friends! I keep some of the best memories from Bolton Health Studio where it all started for all of us across the UK: history was created and many lives involved in keeping fit were changed forever.'

THE NVQ

OUR NABBA COURSE had attracted an enormous amount of attention from the Further Education Authorities who invited us to present our course criteria to various colleges throughout the country. This helped in acquiring the funding to support young people wanting to gain a Vocational Qualification.

Because our courses had been designed to qualify people to work in Health Clubs, we were seen to be an employment enhancement and were delighted with this further recognition. If people did our courses they would put themselves in a much better position to find employment. The support of Oscar and NABBA however, was being challenged. People within the organisation had seen the growth of our business and were waiting in the wings to break out on their own. The general idea was for certain individuals to deliver the courses in their own regional area. The name NABBA Weight Training Instructor Course had become a poacher's target: along with me, Oscar could see the perils of this and how it could all go pear-shaped. The courses would continually progress with the industry continuing to grow. We had now been using the name of NABBA for almost ten years and it had been good for both of us.

Oscar was now starting to suffer ill health at the age of eighty. There was a new breed of people influencing the NABBA executive council and Oscar's role of President would soon be replaced by Ivan Dunbar the Belfast area manager. Ivan and I got on well and shared a mutual respect. We talked at length of how bodybuilding was changing: drugs were becoming a major problem. And just as much of a problem for us, were the other people in NABBA who were setting themselves up to run courses. I knew we were both sensing the relationship was beginning to crumble and the breakup was inevitable.

In due course I received a very personal letter from Oscar explaining his concerns. He was by this time under the doctor on what he described as extreme fatigue and a tired heart. The letter dated 27th November 1990 was written with some despair of how bodybuilding was going and how he was working with little hope of any gratuity from NABBA. He was not relishing his next meeting in just a few days time with the executive committee. I would reflect many times on that letter: the sadness, the despair and lack of respect for such a great,

great man. His letter, in essence foretold the future. When he died on the 21st March 1991 it was a sad time for all who had come to know him over the years. It also signalled the re-naming and re-branding of our courses.

This was the same year our courses won the Government's very prestigious "National Training Award", beating national companies across all industries. Oscar would have been truly delighted to have been at the awards ceremony held in the Queen Elizabeth Halls in London to see us receive the award from Prince Charles.

To Oscar the NABBA courses were a milestone for an organisation he loved. They had added status and respectability. It was a course on the verge of government recognition and supported by thousands who had ambitions to work in the emerging fitness industry. Many people who had never heard of NABBA, who were not bodybuilders, would come along and sit the course to take a qualification that would change their working life.

The signs were already there that fitness and bodybuilding would become separate entities. Ironically the split with NABBA and the passing of Oscar would be the start of a new era for us. All we had to do was change our name, our logo and a little thing called identity – in other words we had to re-brand the company. At this time and with the industry growing rapidly I had become involved in the forming of the FIA (Fitness Industry Association.)

JOHN O'GROATS

THE BBC TV series '40 Minutes' tagged me the Multi-Marathon Man after covering me on my record attempt at running from John O'Groats to Lands End.

I had a call from the BBC's quite brilliant TV interviewer Harold Williamson who had made his reputation filming 'That's Life' with Esther Rantzen and later 'The Man Alive' programmes. He then went on to head the '40 minutes' series which was to cover our epic run. All of this came about because I had previously featured in an earlier programme of 'Man Alive' on the human body. Bolton Health Studio's contribution was to demonstrate how you could change your shape through weight training. Supporting me on that programme were the

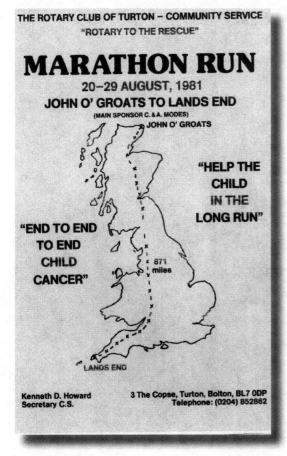

Marathon run.

three heavenly bodies of Bridget Gibbons, Gordon Pasquill and Karen Gilmore.

Bridget would go on to win the Miss Universe, Gordon Pasquill had just won the Junior Mr Europe and Karen Gilmore at the age of forty was in fantastic shape and a mother of five children. Thank goodness I was only doing the talking!

Harold Williamson was always on the lookout for a good story and due to the success of the show it sparked a relationship with him and Bolton Health Studio. He would ring me from time to time asking if there was anything new happening. When I told him I was thinking of running from John O'Groats to Lands End he immediately took an interest and this resulted in the '40 minutes' team coming to Bolton to talk, three months before the programme would go ahead in mid-August.

BBC tv

BRITISH BROADCASTING CORPORATION
KENSINGTON HOUSE RICHMOND WAY LONDON W14 0AX
TELEPHONE 01-743 1272 TELEX: 265781
TELEGRAMS AND CABLES: TELECASTS LONDON TELEX

12th May, 1981.

Dear Doug,

It was good talking to you yesterday and I was delighted to learn that you had as much faith in Ken as I have but, just in case, will you reserve a spare seat for me on your get-away plane!

I'm writing, at your invitation, to say that we are planning to make a documentary film covering the entire run from John O'Groats to Land's End.

As you know this kind of operation, from our end, involves a large expenditure of money and resources and it will only be worth our while if we can be guaranteed, by you, that no other television channel will be allowed to cover the entire run.

Obviously no restriction would be asked as far as local television, radio, or newspaper coverage whose efforts would help boost the appeal, but as far as the entire run is concerned we would require exclusive coverage.

We are aiming at a 40-minute documentary on the trials and tribulations and, expectantly, success of a very brave and exciting venture.

May I look forward to hearing from you at your earliest convenience and may I wish you every success in your own undertaking.

Yours sincerely,

Harold Williamson

Mr. Doug Farnworth,
White House,
Chapeltown Road,
Bromley Cross,

BBC TV Letter.

134

Everything happened very quickly: at the time it was just an idea, with nothing set up. It was an idea that could quite easily have stopped there and then. But it was a different matter now the TV had taken an interest and forces beyond our immediate thoughts were beginning to come into play. After having competed in twenty-six marathons and literally hundreds of other races I was suited to distance running, more slow twitch fibres than fast twitch and I must confess that the thought of attempting a record of such magnitude appealed to me.

I knew I didn't have the anaerobic or explosive capacity, weight training had taught me that. The old saying of 'You can't put in what God left out' in my case was true. Not only was I suited to endurance but I loved doing it. I would think nothing of going out on a Sunday morning to do a thirty mile run (when time permitted.) I still find it hard to believe that even when I was once offered a private plane trip

BBC Multi-Marathon Man.

to LeTouquet in France to have lunch and a look around the town with my friend Michael Smyth, I said,

'I can't come, I have to do my Sunday run.' This was *one* run out of a thousand runs. I guess human nature keeps us gravitating to what we do the best.

Harold's call and subsequent interview set the ball rolling for what was to be a very challenging and extraordinary year. The run from John O'Groats to Lands End would be over 800 miles and I was attempting to cover this in 10 days meaning a run of about 80 miles each day.

I would embark on a training regime that was unbelievably hard and what we called in those days LSD – long slow distance. This in itself was going to be a problem. I had spent the last six years trying to run fast over 10k, half marathons, twenty milers and marathons and

---

MANCHESTER AREA HEALTH AUTHORITY (Teaching) SOUTH DISTRICT
Chairman of the Authority R. B. Prain • District Administrator R. A. Lawson, M.A.

CHRISTIE HOSPITAL & HOLT RADIUM INSTITUTE,
WITHINGTON,
MANCHESTER,
M20 9BX

Telephone:
061-445 8123

AWY/SJ

19th November 1981

Mr K Heathcote
Bolton Health Studios
30 Mawdsley Street
Bolton
Lancs   BL1 1LF

Dear Mr Heathcote

Following last Thursday night, we are writing to formally thank you for the tremendous effort and energy you invested on our behalf in the long run project. The total sum of £25,000 which the Rotary Club of Turton have managed to collect as a result of your run is a magnificent sum and we are very grateful to you for being the "vehicle" upon which the sponsorship could be based.

We particularly enjoyed the BBC forty minutes programme and the alternative version presented on Thursday, and we hope these will provide you with a happy reminder of such an ambitious project.

It would be unfortunate if our personal association with you should end now that the money has been raised and I would like to assure you that you will always be welcome to visit the laboratories to see how the money is being spent and how our research is going along.

Kind regards.

Yours sincerely

Dr D Pearson   Dr S Kumar   A W Yates
Consultant Radiotherapist   Head of Paediatric Research   Deputy Admini

Christie Hospital letter.

now I was going to have to start to run slower, even slower than in normal training.

I also had to plan runs that simulated the distance, runs that would deplete and exhaust: I had to do this, run a business and have a social life.

There was also another criterion; this was not about crazy ideas, ambition or ego satisfaction. This run was going to have to do good for others. The charity I had a keen desire to support was Child Leukaemia and so the decision was made. This charity would play a very important role in the attempt.

Planning something of this magnitude creates a lot of different issues. I had not given much thought to how it would be organised, but once it became known all sorts of things started to happen. A good friend of mine called Dougie Farnworth had heard of what I was attempting to achieve and, it being his year as President of Turton Rotary Club, he decided to put the suggestion to his fellow Turton Rotarians to see if it would appeal to them as much as it appealed to him to get involved and make it their charitable event of that year. This would turn out to be very significant with the whole event falling into the lap of their exceptional organisational abilities.

Dougie would prove to be a huge help in the organisational skills and raising the money. The most satisfactory outcome of the run for me was the £25,000. the run raised which we put into the coffers for research in Child Leukaemia. Even now I still have pangs of guilt that so many people were prepared to put so much effort into supporting this idea of mine.

Sponsoring the run were C & A – a Dutch company department store. The catalyst for this was a friend of ours called Marie Gildea whose brother-in-law Paul Johnson happened at the time to be the Marketing Director. Paul's persuasive powers were responsible for the sponsorship and suddenly we had an event: a full blown publicity machine driven by a small army of supportive, excited and enthusiastic people. BBC TV, Turton Rotary Club, Staff and Members of Bolton Health Studio together with a shedload of people who just wanted to help and be involved.

The planning and involvement together with so much support was extraordinary and quite humbling. Dougie and his fellow Rotarians with their superb organisational skills would now take away all the hassle, thus enabling me to concentrate on getting into shape for the

Long Run. I cannot thank them enough for how they just bought into the whole idea. Thirty years have elapsed but my stomach still churns when I think of the number of people who came forward to support us.

There can be no greater sense of justification of people getting together for a common cause or goal. They would just turn up to ask what they could do to help. They would even offer to run with me and, may I add, much slower than they usually ran. I was even approached by eighty years old Arnold Horsley who lived about a mile away and who would leave me for dead half way up Tottington Road. I don't think Arnold had ever heard of LSD. The whole thing was quite overwhelming.

Quite frankly, if all this support had not happened I would probably have questioned myself about doing it. It was a massive commitment. The run was the least of my worries – I now had all these people with a common cause seemingly caught up in the frenzy and the runner being a sideline. It did not go to that extent, but made me realize just how much we rely on others. This interdependency was a lesson in how a collective force can drive things forward.

THE DAY BEFORE

BRUNO SABINI WOULD say and not without humour, 'I have not seen a pavement for 500 miles!' He and Pat Dolan had just arrived at the John O'Groats Hotel in the far reaches of North Scotland. The whole scene was taking on the appearance of a movie in the making. Along with Bruno and Pat and my back-up team, we had the whole entourage of Rotary, the Christie Hospital, C & A, and the BBC: all were to be involved in covering and supporting my solo world record attempt.

I was now the chap reliant on these five groups: the back-up crew of my business partner Bill Stevenson, my friend and driver of the caravan Mike Smyth, another friend and representative of Turton Rotary, Dougie Farnworth, alongside Bruno. Pat would battle, negotiate, be flawless, a good runner, good pacer, conversationalist and protector of the runner. They would oversee, protect and shelter me from all the other possible infringements and desperately try to keep the runner running.

In the Guinness Book of Records, the run from John O'Groats to Lands End was supposedly 11 days: This would mean running 80 miles each day on 10 consecutive days. Even though they had not been asked, the BBC was covering the run in its entirety. BBC commentator Harold Williamson had every faith in producing a programme that would excite and move the watching public.

By the time dusk had fallen the hotel was full. Everyone was a little apprehensive at the thought of setting off to cover the 780 mile run. A good night's sleep was on the cards for our early rise at 4am to avoid the heavy traffic when coming out of Scotland and also it was meant to establish a habit that would carry us through to the finish.

At 4.55am we were greeted by darkness, high winds and rain: Pat Dolan had drawn the short straw to pace me on this first stint of the day. However, the previous night's attempts of relaxing had somehow got out of hand. His talent for socialising and love of nice Claret accompanied by a good highland steak were the reasons for my mate's absence! We were not to worry; no one had slept well, so it was Bill and I who stepped over the threshold to take those first few steps of many thousands on the journey to Land's End.

We would have the first half hour of running before the first cracks of dawn greeted the two lonely runners. It was a desolate featureless landscape offering little other than the sound of our shoes on the long tarmac road. The words of Bruno would echo back – no pavements – fields with a scattering of sheep, the wind and us.

Running on a road at 5 am in Scotland, there is not a lot of conversation. Bill would do the first 10 miles before handing over to Bruno. The dialogue with runners is usually about the events of the night before, but all of us except for Pat had retired early. The emptiness of our surroundings did little for making conversation, but there was an assurance, a comfort and a companionship that distance runners appreciate when forcing the mind and body to do things they would rather leave alone at this time of the day. For Harold to have some meat for the viewers we had been 'miked up'. Sorry Harold, but we had nothing tasty to say at this stage, we were not thinking that this intrusion would reveal our inner thoughts and anxieties in the miles of the days to come!

Reiss – Wick – Lybster – Latheron – Dumbeth would all slip by – 36.5 miles on the clock; Pat was now over his blip! I knew his reliability in the future would be unquestionable. The miles and the villages would roll by – Helmsdale – Brora – Golspie – 69 miles – Bonar Bridge was our target for the day and, with night time looming we were greeted in the small highland village to a backdrop of bagpipes accompanying a warm and hospitable welcome from the Mayor and High Sheriff, who presented me with a cheque from the local Rotary Club.

Chris Brasher who was the organiser of the first London Marathon and founder of the New Balance Company had fast-tracked with his compliments 6 pairs of shoes. Great shoes, but on reflection had I been wise to change at the last minute from Reebok! Experience over the years had taught me that all brands have their own particular qualities; some may have a slightly broader or narrower sole that has only 1/8th of an inch difference in the heel or it may have a stronger upper and many other smaller idiosyncrasies. But the change from all that training for the event in one brand of shoe could have just tweaked the ankle! At this stage of the run there were no worries, but little did I know the small niggle I was feeling would give me some aggravation in the days that followed. At some time every athlete courts and embraces injury, it is all part of the deal, but if given time and rest most heal themselves.

Tiredness and fatigue is a constant companion of the endurance

Incorrect

He won Distribution Rights in UK for Reebok

runner. The previous seven months had absorbed thousands of miles in the build-up to this run: the legs, ankles, knees, tendons, sinews, muscle and bone had all been hardened to accommodate this very challenging event. There was little question in my mind of not being ready and the tweak of the Achilles tendon was of no concern.

Day 2 would see us up at 4am ready to hit the road at 5. The first 10 miles would take us onto the A9 heading for Inverness and the prophecy of Bruno of long roads with no pavements would be with us once again. I was told later I had been hallucinating, but the one thing that was not a hallucination was a crackpot driver in a speeding delivery van manically forcing us into the thickets which separated the grazing land from the road. Inverness, like the other towns, would come and go; the A9 would give us problems with the steep camber of the road. The shift in balance to the left would put more pressure onto the left increasing the aggravation on the now inflamed tendon.

I had had all kinds of niggling injuries over the previous months, but small adjustments to the daily run would always rectify these anomalies. Running on softer ground, on grass, on a treadmill, or even the odd day off would help. There are many ways to train through many injuries, but here, with tens of miles to run there would be no respite. Behind the scenes and unknown to me the crew were having some concern for my depreciating condition. Still, we carried on; not quite as productively – 160 miles on the clock and 64 miles for the day.

We were now deep into the mountain range of the Cairngorms; the weather could and would change by the minute – cloudy, sunny, warm and even flurries of snow. The unrelenting and undulating A9 with its irritating camber was forcing an ungainly gait to compensate for the inflamed tendon.

In the Scottish Highlands Aviemore is well known for skiing and Father Christmas. It would be here that this bearded man in the month of August who I assumed had come out of hibernation would present us with another cheque – a rare sight and a rare occasion! The miles would continue to roll – Bruar, the pass of Killiecrankie – 213 miles on the clock.

Day 4 saw us leaving the Highlands slowly threading our way through the traffic towards Pitlochry and Perth. It is not just the undulation of the road or the high and low hills and valleys of the country road, but the peaks and troughs of our emotions and the bodily and mental fatigue that engulfs us in utter despair and a tiredness that one minute consumes and then with no logical, physical or even psychological reason the body will overcome this desperate fatigue and rise out of the hopelessness.

This is different from the tiredness of marathons. There is no end, no light at the end of the tunnel, no finishing line and no tape to run through: just the next step and the next mile with the end of the day too far into the future. In contrast, there were lighter moments with Bill, Pat and Bruno lifting these desperate moments. The refreshment stops for fluids were always served by our driver and caravan manager Mike Smythe – a piece of cake and a cup of tea served with humour, conversation and ribald laughter. Mike would have been better used in his business empire back in Bolton, but he chose instead to be a humble servant to 40 year old runners who were expressing jokes more suited to a teen movie.

There also appeared to be some subterfuge going on that was sheltered from me and it would be over 30 years before I would become aware that our back-up car was being bugged! Harold and the producer Desmond Lapsy were hoping I would reveal my trials and tribulations, what I was feeling, where I was in the pain barrier and how much I was suffering. All were of great interest for the 'mic' and the 'invasive eye' of the camera. This was all kept hidden, but what had become apparent were the different agendas that were going on within the different parties and the 'Beeb' ruthlessly searching for the story – a story that that would exclude the Sponsors C & A who had forbidden any advertising on their production.

The Rotary also had their agenda and were doing a brilliant job collecting money as part of this terrific campaign; Christies deployed a doctor to help in supporting us. Not a Doctor of Medicine, but a Doctor of Chemistry. All these different agendas jockeying for time, space, information and all intent on doing what they did best.

The bugging of the car was discovered by Mike and Pat after a deluge of uncouth criticism of Desmond's crew. Not realising the car had a hidden microphone Pat was letting rip on Desmond's team on how they were showing no concern for the central figure. Pat has a well educated talent for bringing everything to the most basic of verbal communication that leaves no one guessing exactly what he means! It didn't put the 'Beeb' out and later it proved to be an example of their professionalism that we would learn to respect and admire.

After leaving the desolate starkness of Northern Scotland, we bathed in the warm sunshine of the beautiful region of Perth and its lush green pastures; on better days and under different circumstances these would have been appreciated more!

In spite of the injury we were still on track for passing the 300 mile mark and it was here we met up with Robert Jelski who joined us from the Isle of Man where he had just raised £2,800 by doing an end to end of the Island.

Support was now arriving from far and wide as we ran into the more built-up areas. After Perth our route would take us through Kinross, Kelty, Crossgates and into Inverkeithing, a town where Pat Dolan would come to live in the years ahead. Leaving these behind, we were now heading for a landmark and a symbol of achievement that both the 'Beeb' and us would see as one of the milestones to pass and enjoy – The Forth Bridge! This was the place the BBC had pinned their hopes on – now they had a story!

Some years later, Dougie Farnworth would tell me that the 'Beeb' would have been happy to have me break down at this stage as there was enough in the can to produce the film. The crossing of the bridge was not only a landmark, but something the team wanted to shoot in daylight. Unfortunately for them my arrival was in the dark and the £30,000 they had spent on a helicopter to film this epic part of the run had mostly gone to waste.

Funnily enough I was feeling quite chirpy, if that is the right expression. However little the 'Beeb' had got out of me, crossing the bridge was a huge pick-up for us – 278 miles and not far from arriving in England.

With the bridge behind us we were now heading through Edinburgh and into the Lowlands. Shaun O'Donnell, a Bolton United Harriers star of track and field would join us: Shaun was an amazing athlete, decathlon, shot-putter, discus, four hundred metre man, all events that contradict the ability of distance running. Not only did he run distance with me, but quite phenomenally he completed the marathon distance on five consecutive days. He actually took five days off from his job as a fireman to join this crazy man who could not have appreciated it more!

The ankle or should I say the Achilles heel was now swelling to 3 times its natural size and to compensate I had been running more flat-footed. Something we were not aware of then, is that the higher the heel, the less pressure is placed on the Achilles tendon and a simple wedge in the shoe could have alleviated this. So, a tip for all budding distance runners, at the first sign of inflammation put a wedge in your shoe.

On the fifth day Brenda arrived in the Lowlands to greet us. Harold and Desmond saw this as a great opportunity to lighten the load! Later, on TV and to the music of Mozart's Piano Concerto we would be filmed running towards each other and embracing. The scene could have been something out of any epic love story, but in true life not really appropriate when every muscle and sinew is crying out for rest. Still, in the words of show biz troopers, 'The show must go on' and whatever was lurking in the deep recesses of my mind I quite spontaneously quipped for the six million viewers watching and listening that running from John O'Groats to Land's End would qualify me to be a eunuch! But the appearance of Brenda made me feel a whole lot better.

On crossing the border into England we experienced mixed feelings; on one hand we had almost 350 miles in the bag; on the other, we knew I would not be able to run through the injury. With just 6 days behind us the accumulation of injuries totalled more than over the last 5 years and even today I still refuse to analyse why! In life, we do what we do, with no one knowing what will happen after the decision has been made.

A former International runner, Jack Haslam, came on board to help me through the bad patches, but instead of helping was judged to be pushing me a little too hard. The time wasn't favourable for Jack, his coming on board caused some resentment from my back-up crew as they continued to protect me, and Jack's three day inclusion would come to a conclusion in Warrington. Even to this day I still do not know why he departed at that time. Jack has now passed on, but I still have a high regard for this friend with whom I spent hours and hours and mile upon mile in training and racing.

Carlisle United F.C. sent their physio out to try and help with my injuries; a new strapping and splint were added, but I could not run with this in place. He said if I had been one of his players I would have been out for six weeks. Well, for us to be out for six hours was impossible, so on we went, winding our way towards the Lakes and Shap.

The gradual climb out of Penrith was defining in more ways than one: Shap was to be another milestone, 410 miles and we were nearing the half-way point. Shap stands at 1200 feet. The gradients vary from steady to severe, some areas being 1 in 6. We arrived in the dark after being on the road for fifteen hours, finishing the day on legs not recovered from the previous day and still nursing the injury to the right ankle. In training and at any other time this stretch of road would have taken thirty minutes, but had now taken double that time.

It was at this point I would once again become aware of how ruthless the TV people could be: the journey from the top of Shap after the day's running completed, I was ferried back by car to the Shap Hotel for our overnight stay. The cameraman Pat O'Shea had already raced back to the hotel and was in waiting: the end of the day's running, the exhaustion, despair and acute tiredness the target for his camera. Arriving in Dougie's car at the front door of the hotel, Pat O'Shea's dramatic shot would see me looking out of the passenger seat window with the crew crowding round the car, immobile and unable to open the car door. The tracksuit top with the C & A logo was an obstacle Pat could not show and at this stage and being in no fit state to understand his next words would come as a surprise, when he said,

'Take off your top and I will never ask anything of you again.' With the mind dull and uncomprehending, the need for food and rest, I slipped out of the tracksuit top to provide Pat with a perfect shot of a man at the end of his tether – white T shirt, a lined and haggard face, ghostlike and a perfect contrast to the dark interior – Pat had got his shot!

Our overnight stay at the Shap Hotel would during the evening see the arrival of my GP Dave Thomas. Dave was a member of our club, a squash player and occasional training partner. He had made the 100 mile trip from Bolton to examine the Achilles and give his opinion. His advice was very much as we had expected – 'Do not continue with the run' – but being well aware of my history he knew full well I would not heed a word of what he said! As a member of a local Amateur Dramatic Association he was enjoying his cameo in the bedroom of my hotel: with the cameras rolling he delivered his lines and milked the opportunity for all it was worth. There is no holding back these show-biz people – great fun. However, we were extremely grateful for our doctor's opinion and the trouble he had taken to make the 200 mile round trip. Dave knew enough about my idiosyncrasies and it was good to see him, but his visit would be the butt of some humour for the remainder of the run after prescribing some anti-inflammatories too big to swallow and destined for the other end. The humour surrounding this minor altercation of human need and necessity would hold no bounds, it was a welcome distraction for all from the 'Beebs' pursuit of pain.

The suppositories did their job! The descent down from the summit of Shap to the town of Kendal was the steepest of the run. Once again we would hit the road at 5.00am and by 6.00 with the anti-flams working we were enjoying a fine English summer morning, the progress and the running better than it had been for some time. I would later be joined by the legendary Great Britain Rugby star Billy Beaumont who would run twenty miles with me through Lancaster. Now we had hit Lancashire, runners were joining us by the dozen. The weather was sunny and warm with clear blue skies and even if it was only a temporary condition I was back to running well. A whole host of runners from Bolton United Harriers would come in and join the ever growing group, an ever increasing tribe of encouragement – great when doing the running – not so great when the culmination came at the Tickled Trout in Preston.

Our day's run would finish on the south side of Preston at Bamber Bridge. With another 68 miles in the can after a good days running, the pain was a little less but the tiredness like a ton of bricks.

This was the time the five groups from the five organisations would converge at the hotel. After being run back to the Tickled Trout by car we were greeted with a staggering amount of people and for the first time in seven days we became aware of just how much interest the run had generated and equally how much involvement there was with the five groups.

The run had reached carnival proportions with each of the groups attracting a huge following and it was hard to judge who had invited who. In attendance for another presentation of cheques, we had the Mayor of South Ribble and the Mayor of Preston, local and national radio, local newspapers from Preston and our own Bolton Evening News. There were runners from Bolton Harriers and other various clubs. The hotel was packed: representatives from C & A, Rotary and Christies. Everywhere full to capacity: the conference room, corridors, bars and restaurants were a mass of people, with the noise reaching fever pitch. After a shower and changing, I came down to join the family in the restaurant for something to eat only to discover there was no food left. No food for the runner! The hotel finally managed to rustle up some food and I finally broke from the hyper-activity to make my way back to the room to try and get some sleep only to be followed by Pat O'Shea who wanted to see the swollen feet and legs.

On my way to the room I bumped into Dennis Lee, a colleague from my running club.

He asked me with some empathy how I was coping. I replied with an equal amount of despair, 'It's like a circus; all I need is a white stallion.'

The start of day eight was just another day at the office! Up at four and on the road at five. There were just a handful of people appearing for the early morning start. However, there was to be some drama ahead. We left the A6 and moved on to the A49. This road would take us through Standish and Wigan before cutting through Newton-le-Willows to Warrington.

Warrington was to be the place where I would rest. Mike Smyth had located a lay-by adjacent to a pub on the outskirts of the town centre and this is where he would park up. There was a lot of activity going on outside with Desmond, his crew, my lads, Pat, Bruno, Bill and Jack and a few others wandering about and wondering what was happening.

By now I was in the caravan talking to Dougie when suddenly there was a commotion outside: with the noise, the cameras started whirring and above the noise someone was shouting, Jack's wife had arrived and parked just in front of the caravan and was still sat in her car. What I wasn't aware of was Jack had come over all wobbly and was trying to explain this to the back-up team, just then an old chap was trying to get into the pub but due to the commotion he couldn't get through! He started to shout, 'We don't ol wi that er in Warrington' as he was trying to get in for his first pint of the day! Suddenly and without any warning he started to clobber Jack with his stick leaving Jack looking a little bewildered. It would only last a matter of seconds before Jack made his escape to the waiting car and his wife. He would take his leave from the run that day due to some kind of stomach upset and what with the heat, the activity, the hustle and bustle it came as no surprise. It was sad to see him go, but Harold and Desmond had captured something unexpected on camera – an old chap clobbering with his walking stick one of our back-up crew. Our commandeering of the pub entrance was a mistake we wouldn't make again – well not in Warrington!

By now the ankle had become so inflamed it was apparent that not just the ankle but sheer fatigue would take over; it was not just me, it was everyone! The back-up team – the BBC crew – and everyone who had done the distance were shattered; they were lacking in sleep, energy and emotionally drained. Pat O'Shea summed it up with one shot of the camera when we were nearing the end: he had caught me asleep in the caravan. Mike had previously warmed up some soup and halfway through, I had fallen asleep, something I hadn't done on any other day. Mike's words in the interview with Harold were,

'I have seen him age 20 years and then recover, I have seen him in the depths of despair and come back again, but this time I haven't got the heart to wake him.'

I would carry on running and coming to an island late in the afternoon when for no apparent reason I followed the sign for Shrewsbury instead of Kidderminster. No one checked the error and I was to finish up being picked up in the car and driven back to re-align the route. Being totally exhausted both mentally and physically and injured in a multitude of places, hips, back, thighs and knees, all brought on by that small tendon above the heel joining the foot bone to the leg bone – a particular bone of contention had brought the lot down!

It was a sad moment when I made the decision to stop at 559 miles. Everyone had given their all; Dougie Farnworth for me was the hero. His commitment and desire to make it work were without compare. Dougie must have covered literally thousands of miles shooting ahead in the car to set up collections, arrange meetings with County Sheriffs, Town Mayors, the Press, sorting out accommodation, looking after the crew, warding off the BBC, liaising with Christies, C & A, the Rotary Clubs along the route and something he never mentioned: that along with Mike Smyth they had both put money into the support team. He is a true and modest, unassuming hero.

Throughout my life I have competed in hundreds of events: I have run thirty, forty and fifty milers and competed in twenty-six marathons and only failed to finish twice; the first time was in a twenty-four hour race and with twelve hours and eight-four miles on the clock I walked away from the track. The second was with nine days and 559 miles on the clock. Was I disappointed at not finishing what I had set out to do in running from Land's End to John O'Groats – you bet I was! But I would not beat myself up. You can only give your best in life and if that's not enough for others, then tough, but I can live with it.

Thirty-seven years after the event Bill Stevenson, Pat Dolan, Bruno

Sabini, Michael Smyth and Dougie Farnworth all remain friends. I salute them all.

I knew by day eight it would be coming to an end and I think everyone else did too. The decision was made on that day and there would be little time spent thinking of how to explain to this incredibly devoted team and later to Harold, Desmond and Pat O'Shea that the whole thing had become more than the runner! We would say little about the running but a lot about human endeavour, compassion and togetherness.

Even now more than thirty years on I still feel emotion: not just for me, but for everyone who committed themselves to the cause. We were all so desperately tired, and concealing all these emotions from Harold and his team, knowing it would be shown to an audience of millions was the hardest task of all. The satisfaction was we had given our all and nobody can do more than that.

Later the stories would come out! The turn-around of the "Beeb" and Desmond, saying it was the best piece of TV he had ever done, turned the ruthlessness to empathy and admiration.

The follow-up celebration dinner at the Last Drop Hotel with all five groups paying tribute to the cause was quite astonishing. The back room staff from the cutting room presented Brenda with a specially edited edition of the run; this cut showed Brenda supposedly swinging from a chandelier in our Health Club and being rescued by Superman (me) as he crashed through a hotel window. The two lads chatting to her were from the cutting room and it appeared they were now like old friends, having spent more time with her than with me. This was a great gesture and a most unusual thing for the 'Beeb' to do.

The vast amount of people involved, together with the money raised for Child Leukaemia, forged friends forever and proved perhaps to be the biggest reward of all.

THE PREP

THE PREPARATION STARTED on 1st January 1986, seven months prior to the Long Run: My plan was to build up in stages. This would mean running moderate to long distance in the first three weeks of every month and adding extra mileage on the fourth week. With six months of training ahead I built up to running about 400 miles each month before easing down during the final three to four weeks.

There are always questions to ask and the big one is:

'How do I get the balance right?'

Not too much and certainly not too little.

To go into something like this is without rehearsal and there will always be a doubt of whether we push too hard and break down or do too little and be unprepared. It has to be right!

With the BBC showing interest there was now a sense of urgency. The dynamics would change; it had become more than two or three people talking whilst out on a training run. This could get serious.

The normal weekly running of eighty to one hundred miles when preparing for a marathon took on a different slant. It was now about quantity not quality. Training for a Marathon is a combination of long slow distance and the pace at about 60-70% maximum, the other 30% is divided between hard and steady running; 80% effort with hard demanding running for about 5% of the weekly total – I called this training in the red. There would be none of this, no intensity, no raging fire, just a slow burn for all of the six months.

Running twenty or thirty miles at a time was not a chore. Regularly throughout the year on a Sunday morning, there was nothing better than setting out to run across the Jumbles Country Park. This beautiful area of hills, trees, water and winding paths presented a different training run on any day of the week. Climbing up from the park I would head out over to Affetside and a vantage point which would open up the views to Manchester, Rivington, Holcombe and Darwen: a vast landscape rich with multi-shades of green, abundant with wildlife of rabbit, fox and deer that stretched to the towns and cities – a feast for the eyes, soul and senses.

After dropping down into The Two Brooks Valley I would meander across to Holcombe Tower, climbing once more to one of the highest peaks in the area before finding a path on the South side of Holcombe

Moor – this was my favourite part of the run: solitude, breathtaking scenery and a stillness that was only broken by the sound of birds, sheep or stream. This would be my sign to stop, take a breather and even a mouthful of water from the spring. This was not training, it was something different: something that belonged just to me, an unexplainable phenomenon and a connection with nature.

I would move on from the moor following the roads and routes leading to both the Entwistle and Wayoh Reservoirs before climbing Turton Moor – another landmark that never ceased to intrigue me. A Witches' Circle and second stop pause making me wonder what these stones had meant to people in the past. In years to follow when running gave way to hiking I would follow the same routes to enjoy the same scenes and bathe in the same emotions that filled the heart, every nerve and sinew.

The descent from the Moor would take me past the ancient building of Turton Towers and the climb back up Chapeltown Road to our home for a most welcome shower and cup of tea. More running miles in the bank and on the clock, the day not yet touched.

There were good days and not so good days training for the long run: good weather and weather that saps your energy levels, your rhythm and moods. Discipline is the key: a little voice says 'another day' knowing full well giving way is not an option.

January saw an accumulation of four-hundred miles: sixteen miles every day for six days with the traditional long run on a Sunday. Slow and steady over the first few months to build background, an ability to soak up the miles and give resilience to muscles, tendons and joints

In February over the same period of time I increased this to 450 or even 500 miles, the same pattern, but a longer run at the weekend. When time permitted I slotted extra miles in on one of the middle days of the week with an easy day following to give some respite.

There were many days when I had to go out and run on tired legs that had not recovered from the previous day's training, but this was in preparation for August.

March was to be a crucial month signalling the end of winter, and with the promise of better weather ahead I would try more ultra distance – sixty or seventy miles at a time with twenty and thirty the following day. My runs taking me from Bolton to Southport or maybe Bolton to Blackpool and back, this gave me a total of 500 or 600 miles in the thirty days.

April, May and June followed the same slow and steady pattern gathering more miles on the fourth week. We also did a dress-rehearsal in June running from Penrith in the Lake District to finish at the Tickled Trout in Preston, a total of eighty-five miles all on the back of the steady mileage done during the week.

In May there was the Three Point Challenge: Run – Work – Home or if you like, Home – Work – Run. Each of these held equal parity; our children Paul and Karen were both at an age of maturing; Paul was already building his career in the catering industry as a Chef; we had made a commitment to support and further his education by taking him once a month to eat at a restaurant of his choice, a decision costing us an arm and a leg over the following months, but well worth the effort. We also visited and dined at restaurants where he

1986 – A training run crossing the old iron bridge of the Jumbles reservoir during a drought.

was employed to learn his trade. These included the much renowned Sharrow Bay on Lake Ulleswater, The Connaught in London and LeManoir aux Quat'Saisons in Oxfordshire, an education that would reward him with a much coveted Michelin star.

High cuisine and long distance running are not exactly compatible, but somehow we managed to make it work. On one occasion when Brenda and I were staying at Sharrow Bay I had the privilege of running in some of the most beautiful countryside in the world. This however, had to coincide with a week of low mileage.

By this time our daughter Karen had now completed her training in Beauty Therapy and after gaining experience working in a salon in Huddersfield she returned to Bolton to work and successfully run the Beauty Salon we had created within the confines and business of Bolton Health Studio.

Negotiating this part of our lives and accommodating the challenges and my compulsion to fulfil this particular event, described by some as a crackpot idea, we did it as a family and even now some forty years later there is still that close-knit mentality.

The balancing of working, long distance running and life is incredibly difficult: our club in Bolton was probably at its peak in 1986. We had in the region of 2000 members, equating to maybe 500 visits a day, every one of these members receiving the very best of service. Exercise classes were branded as 'Ken Heathcote's Fitness Class' and 'Fatigues' – much like the 'Boot Camp' classes of today. Both of these were put onto audio tape and sold with an exercise chart or booklet as part of the package. I would also instruct and take eight or nine classes a week with up to forty people participating. There would be staff breakfast meetings, marketing and sales, my involvement with the 'Industry Lead Body' and 'Fitness Industry Association' – both of these operating out of London: all had to be dovetailed into our daily lives whilst fitting in the training for the 'Long Run.'

Strange as it may seem, I thrived on all of this. Brenda and I did manage to have a break at times; we had friends who we socialised with and we ate out most Friday nights for close on twenty years, a ritual that treated us to the most exquisite food, courtesy of our son's education. There were a few occasions due to the nature of my life when I would frequently fall asleep during dessert! I was informed later in life by Gabbi, Paul's wife, but his girlfriend at that particular time, that the front of house staff would take bets on who nodded off first, me or our friend Michael. All this was, of course, when we ate where Paul was cooking at that time.

In truth my whole life revolves around Brenda; and as I write this in longhand she will be the one who sits at the computer to type and do the first edit before it goes on to be scrutinised and proof read and returned for more editing and typing. Like most things in life we can never exist alone.

My target was to reach four hundred miles in the last week of June: a week that would see me running seventy miles every day. This would be the final push before easing back during July and what remained into August.

That final week in June would literally mean getting up at 5am and running throughout the day. I still went into the club to oversee the day's duties, but in essence, it was just run and eat, with short inter-mittent rests until I had clocked up the quota for the day. The strategy was simple, just keep running.

JOHNSON FOLD AND 50th BIRTHDAY

How to Eat an Elephant

THE BEAUTIFUL WEST Pennine Moors are separated from the main range by the Irwell Valley. The moorlands include Withnell, Anglesarke and Rivington. In the extreme west are Darwen and Turton Moor and further afield Oswaldtwistle and Holcombe. Central to all the moors and standing at a height of 1,496 feet is the main spine of Winter Hill, the highest point of all the moors.

This area is of some historical importance with evidence of human activity dating back to Neolithic times, a place and time long gone with different wants, needs and values.

With this backdrop on the edge of Bolton we have the Johnson Fold Council Estate. This is just like any other estate in the country with perhaps one exception: in front of the Primary School playground

Ken with Des Drummond and Peter Reid.

155

stands an all weather floodlit soccer pitch which is now twenty-seven years old and unique in the fact that it carries no hint of damage, graffiti or vandalism, something the residents of the estate are immensely proud of.

The reason for this minor miracle is all down to one man: a youth worker by the name of Gerry Luczka who was employed by the Local Authority.

Gerry had a dream and a vision for this all-weather pitch to be built on the estate: he said it would reduce and even eliminate the problems that were continually tormenting the residents of Johnson Fold.

The year was 1981: crime was at an all time high with gangs of youths rampaging across the estate and the police being so stretched they struggled to keep order.

Gerry had started to liaise with the residents' committee, a small group of people who had come up with an idea for raising money to help get this all weather pitch started.

Raising the money was proving more difficult than expected and after a year they had only managed to get a little over £2000. In the meantime, Gerry was working on securing grants and sourcing money through the local authority, the Sports Council and the Playing Fields Association. He was also putting together the cost and a list of companies who could build this facility. All this was taking time and the longer it went on the more difficult it became for the residents to raise funds.

When Gerry finally had everything in order he met with the committee to tell them the cost of building this all-weather pitch

On court with Jill Wallwork.

would be in the region of £90,000. This is when the campaign would nearly came to an end! It was an almost unreachable amount of money with the local authority and other organisations wanting something more than just the idea. The worst was yet to come: the doubting Thomas's saying it could not work. What about maintenance? What about vandalism? Even the teachers at the primary school were now objecting, saying it would restrict playing space. Gerry was not to be deterred.

By 1984 the hard working residents' committee were about to give up and Gerry knew he had to come up with some answers. The project needed a boost.

One evening and just by chance he was looking through the Bolton Evening News when he read an article about my up and coming 50th birthday. I was going to repeat what I had done on my 40th but in numerals of fifty by running fifty miles, lifting 50,000lbs in a series of exercise in fifty minutes, play five people at squash and then finish with 500 sit ups. He immediately saw an opportunity that could help them raise more money.

A programme from one of the organised events.

Gerry Luczka and me at the opening of the Johnson Fold Artificial Pitch in 1986.

Gerry Luczka and me in 2013 at the still pristine Johnson Fold Pitch.

The very next day whilst waiting in a queue at the bank who should walk in and approach me but Gerry Luczka. I listened to what he had to say and immediately identified with what he wanted to do. The picture he painted of the Johnson Fold Estate resonated with my youth. I could almost feel the despair the residents were experiencing.

I asked him how this would work for him. Why would my efforts motivate people like the Local Authority, the Football Association or the Sports Council? I don't think anyone but he knew the answers. But all would unfold and become obvious when he and the residents committee launched The Ken Heathcote Youth Appeal.

THE KEN HEATHCOTE YOUTH APPEAL

THE REAL SUCCESS of this was due not just to Gerry and the residents' committee, but also to the total involvement of people on the estate. The kids, the mums and dads and the local police who had all previously shown no interest were now asking how they could help and get involved. There was now a purpose and a passion. They were now seeing what we had been trying to accomplish for so long.

Gerry is not a businessman, but he is not without enterprise. All sorts of wonderful ideas were now forming in his head and being put into action. The project was gaining momentum, with the influential Councillor David Dingwall quoted as saying this was something that had been needed for a long time.

Almost by magic, money allocated for sport on different grants started to materialise. The residents were organising sponsored pram pushing and bingo. The local bobbies raised over £1000 with a sponsored bike ride. It was as though the whole town had been galvanised into doing something for this estate.

A great success was the Gala Night: a concert sponsored by Michael Smyth of the Radcliffe Road Garage Group and backed by the Bolton Wanderers Board of Directors. The concert drew on the local celebrities of comedian Stu Francis, folk singer Bob Williamson, Tony Berry of the Houghton Weavers, song writer/pianist Howard Broadbent, vocalist Jo Crompton and the appearance of soccer stars Frank Worthington and Peter Reid. The entry fee for this fantastic evening was the paltry sum of £1. But it ensured a full house and a hugely successful evening.

A charity football match was also arranged between a Manchester and Liverpool Select Eleven with names like Sandy Saddler, Tony Dunn, Ian St John, Roger Hunt and many others taking part to help this deprived estate.

The whole campaign was now in full swing. It would be many years later that I would ask Gerry the question what was the catalyst.

Without any hesitation he answered that the key issue was the people on the estate. He also said 'the money is always there, it just needs accessing.'

The collective efforts of the estate triggered the required funding, but he said,

'What we now need is some presence – and that presence is Ken Heathcote.'

The sporting theme of running, lifting and squash all identified with the sport of soccer and an activity centre that would give access to kids three hundred and sixty-five days a year.

All that was left for me to do was to get out there and do it!

This is how Gerry Luczka would describe it....

Members of the Johnson Fold Community had been fund raising for 14 months and I began to sense that morale was beginning to wane. Lots of wonderful little initiatives had taken place but our target of £10,000 was a long way off being reached. At this point residents had raised £2,300 and although this was a fantastic achievement the target was a long way off. I couldn't help thinking that we needed a high profile event to re-invigorate the campaign and quickly reach our target.

One Tuesday evening, while I was reading the Bolton Evening News, I came across an article which captured my attention. Local gym owner Ken Heathcote was going to attempt a muscle marathon on his 50th birthday. He was going to run 50 miles, lift 50,000 lbs in 50 minutes, play five games of squash and finish off by doing 500 sit ups. ALL IN ONE DAY!!! 'Wow,' I thought, 'That will take some doing.' But what really got me interested was that he was looking to raise a substantial amount of money, through sponsorship and donations and give it all to a local charity.

Any local charity interested in being considered needed to contact Ken. This was just what we were looking for. The following day I was driving through town and needed to call into the bank. As I was in the process of completing my withdrawal slip another customer walked in and stood next to me. As I looked across and much to my amazement I noticed it was Ken Heathcote. I introduced myself and explained that I'd read his article and briefly told him about our project.

Two days later I met Ken at Bolton Health Studio, gave him lots more information and he agreed to choose us as his charity. We decided to call Ken's muscle marathon 'The Ken Heathcote Youth Appeal.'

Fundraising was rejuvenated and 6 months later a total of £9,500 had been raised.

The 'Ken Heathcote Youth Appeal' played such an important part in the realisation of this project. I would go as far as to say that it was the 'catalyst' which provided the much needed impetus at a crucial point of the fundraising.

THE 50TH

SO HERE I was again ten years later, ten years older and about to have another go!

The starting time was 6.45am. The weather was good and I had just had a cup of tea and two slices of toast. Remarkably, people had actually come down to the Town Hall Square in Bolton to see me off or should it be cheer me on!

A running pal of mine Graham Bennison, who was a Primary School Head Teacher, would not just set off with me, but would run the whole distance of fifty miles and with no apparent preparation. He had a relaxed economical running style, his arms carried low, very little lift on the trailing leg, relaxed shoulders and easy pace, all so important on runs like this. He would be a great help.

The fifty miles took a little less than seven and half hours to bring us back to the starting point on the square. All the lifting equipment was ready and set up for the next discipline with Ian Thorpe's single station pulley machine ready for the next exercise.

It was a warm and sunny afternoon with just the right temperature. The Sunday shoppers around the square were not really aware that the event was going on, but it was an added attraction for their day out. To raise more money for the charity Gerry had also organised a Bouncy Castle, a coconut shy and games for the children.

A friend of Gerry's had brought along a TV crew to film the whole event which some months later would be shown on Screen Sports.

The run went with no incident but, like all ultra distance runs there are lapses of energy. The blood sugar may drop or concentration may go. Running fifty miles is not a big deal if your preparation has been good. With seven months of training in place my physical aspect was sound. I would follow the same circuit and system of exercises as I had done on my 40th. Upper body work utilising a peripheral heart action – working hard on one muscle group and then switching to another. It was all going well: no one collapsing, no dramatic occurrences: the secret, like the run, was to work within the limits. This was something I had discovered when running marathons. The pace is vital to performance – mind you, I had run a few marathons that had taken me to my very limit – virtually seconds away from total wipe out. Not this time though, I paced the 50,000 lbs in fifty minutes perfectly.

In 1985 Anne Hobbs was the British No 2 tennis player. In the same year Des Drummond was playing for Leigh and Great Britain in Rugby League. Jill Wallwork was the doubles Badminton Champion and Peter Reid was playing soccer with Everton and England. My fifth opponent in my five games of squash was Bob Harvey a very accomplished Squash Pro. After just completing eight hours of continuous exercise I was to come face to face with all of these.

When doing events like this balance is difficult: the run is all about aerobic exercise. The lifting is a combination of anaerobic and aerobic. The short sharp bursts of speed and continuous movement deplete the muscles differently again. Five opponents one after the other would test the best and the worst of my abilities.

There was no question about this being just five games of squash and going through the motions. I fully intended to compete with them all – mind you, they weren't all good squash players!

Peter Reid played squash like he played soccer – full throttle – hard, aggressive and totally committed. Fortunately for me, he was not as good at squash as at football.

Peter was a fantastic player who played for Bolton Wanderers, Everton, Manchester City and England in the World Cup.

I guess Peter underestimated me as our game went to five sets, but whether by accident or design I managed to pip him in the fifth.

It didn't go as well with Anne – she was a class act and boy did she make me work! I tried desperately to win a game, but she beat me in the end 9-7 9–6 9-7. At this stage I had been on court one and a half hours and still had three more opponents to face.

Tennis and squash compliment each other, but not so much badminton: I was meant to be playing Jill's husband Brian, a British champion, who I had known for many years, but he was unable to make it on the day, so I had to contend with his super athletic wife who was a fabulous badminton player. Squash did not suit Jill and this was one I won.

Des Drummond was next up: he was the greatest national athlete I have ever met. At the time he was playing for his club Leigh and also touring the world playing for Great Britain: I had trained him for the British TV series of Superstars in which he was narrowly beaten in the World Series. I noticed that the guy who won had cheated in the squat thrusts – his feet not leaving the floor. His arms were also not fully locked on the parallel bar dips. Des without a doubt would have won the World Series if everything had been equal. What an athlete and now I had to face him at squash.

Fortunately for me Des was not a good squash player. Like Peter he had all the attributes for his chosen sport, but somehow this did not fuse into the game of squash. I managed to squeeze a 3 -2 win in a wild, windmill-like game.

It was now seventeen games and one more opponent to go: Fatigue was beginning to take its toll and this time I had a very proficient player to contend with.

Lactic acid is the substance that suffuses the muscles when they become fatigued. We see it often when watching sport on TV – soccer players lying on their back with a colleague pushing the foot back to stretch the cramping calf muscle. Tennis players being massaged between sets, delaying the oncoming spasms of oxygen deprived limbs. Total immobility as the marathon runner hits the mysterious wall of mental and physical limits, unable to sum up another step – energy, glycogen and will all drained, the tank empty, reserves spent, nothing left. I hadn't quite reached that point but I was getting very close and with one game left I was starting to get worried.

My final opponent would be Bob Harvey. He was an excellent touch player and even when fresh I hated going on court with touch players.

After completing twelve hours of continual exercise I was thinking just go on and get it over with, but I could not let go and it went to five. With my blood sugar at an all time low I hated Bob's style, I hated the game and I hated the fact that he could not finish me off. When you are in a competitive mood all this goes through the mind and you will do almost anything to win. This is why top class athletes today train so hard with their fitness levels taking them beyond the limits. It was not so in the past and it was not uncommon to see them collapse at the end of a run or event. The fitness levels of the athletes of today overcome that and we reach the limit before the moment of collapse. I got through those last five sets only because my fitness prevented collapse.

Another condition we see more of today is how quickly athletes and sportsmen recover: recovery levels are an indication of how fit they are. This is reflected in top class competitive sports such as tennis, soccer, swimming and athletics. These demand all year round fitness. Of course there is a price to pay with the athlete having a shorter career span which is usually brought on by injuries that in most cases fail to heal.

That last game with Bob was about as near as I'll get to falling over, something the sceptics would have relished! But I didn't because I was fit enough to attack the last discipline of 500 sit ups without making too much of a fuss.

The five disciplines had taken 12 hours 20 minutes: hundreds of people had got involved and the event had engaged the community in the most positive way. It is said, it is not the winning but the taking part. But by taking part we had all won.

The real winner was not the residents, the police or the volunteers of the youth appeal: it was the youth worker who had hustled, lobbied, scrounged and persuaded me and others to put themselves forward for an incredibly worthwhile cause.

The politicians should look at this model – these things make a difference – these things will have a positive effect on people's lives. They create purpose, community, engagement, togetherness and hope. They provide a goal, a vision and a mission that did not exist before.

Twenty-eight years later the all weather floodlit soccer pitch on the Johnson Fold Estate is still in use – not just in use, but flourishing. It is vandal-free and still providing a service to the community. One youth worker said to me:

'Barring a small minority, all the young people on the estate are engaged in some activities.' It is something other estates in the Bolton area are lacking, in other words, an estate less troublesome than others.

The kids who were using this all weather pitch twenty-eight years ago are now adults. In 2013 a new generation is taking advantage of this facility and this will go on year after year. The famous Liverpool Manager Bill Shankley was asked if he thought football was a matter of life and death.

'No' was his reply, 'Football is more important than death.'

The all weather pitch at Johnson Fold Estate is living proof of what Shankley meant.

In early evening in all kinds of weather when heading along the ring road just past Moss Bank Park you will see a glow emanating from a position just in front of Johnson Fold Primary School. The box like compound is surrounded by a high interlinked fence. I sometimes stop to look across and watch the bobbing heads of young people expelling energy. I watch carefully and if lucky I catch sight of a football and hear the music of the kids at play.

The glow of light is a testament of hope, a beacon that shouts

'Look at me, see what I am doing, listen to me, this is good, this is right, come to me and play.'

I nod and acknowledge and think 'Hey I helped to make that happen.' Gerry Luczka, the people of the Johnson Fold Estate and yes, me.

The Prep

When I started training back in 1950, Jim Halliday gave me the best piece of advice I ever had on preparation. See yourself winning, come right back to the moment and then take that first step on the ultimate journey.

It seems strange that the advice came from a powerhouse of a weightlifter whose sport was totally dependent on short, sharp bursts of strength. But, it is not about the sport, it is about the preparation and taking a further step: it is not about the physical dynamics of the sport or the event, but about the mental approach.

Preparing to run fifty miles, lift 50,000 lbs in fifty minutes, followed by five competitive games of squash and finishing with 500 sit ups is 85% mental, yes, even crazy, but that 85% is between the ears! As Jim would say, you lock the event in your mind, and then start the journey.

My journey started nine months prior to the idea of repeating what I had done on my 40th. Ten years later and ten years older the idea had been floating around in my subconscious when reaching forty-nine.

Feeling that my pace had slowed I stopped racing marathons after the London: the John O'Groats had also come and gone and with twenty-six marathons, three twenty-four hour races and twenty-four races of fifty, sixty and seventy miles under my belt my mind was turning to the ultra-distance scene.

Distance did not faze me: fifty miles was just another day running. The real problem arising was the mixing of aerobic and anaerobic stuff and the preparation. Another major problem was fitting it all in with my day-to-day business.

A typical day started at 5 am: I set out and ran for an hour finishing the run at the club. Showered and changed I then slotted a session in on the weights and if time permitted a session on the squash court would follow. On occasions when time allowed I would put in more mileage, more time in the gym and more time on the squash court. Many times I worked a fourteen hour day fitting the training in when time permitted.

There were also times when I spent the whole day practising the disciplines. Anyone running a small business will know the difficulty of time, staff, money and day to day procedures that demand the customers' attention. My philosophy in business was we had to be there for the customer and that strategy also included me. Everything had to be arranged around that. The 50th was a simple matter of stepping up a gear and more than anything changing the mindset.

Friday evenings were reserved for socialising and eating out with our friends Michael and Margaret Smyth: inevitably it would always be at a good restaurant, meaning at least two hours at the table with someone not always staying awake.

The heavy demands of business together and training meant leading a seriously controlled and disciplined existence, but it was something that gave me a great deal of satisfaction. The plan was to keep mixing the disciplines with a key part to stay just below the edge, but if a rest day was need I would take it. Being fit and just below peak fitness was the real secret to this with my mantra always being consistency – even without special events.

The real plus was I had done it all ten years earlier: the questions were, 'Can I do it now that I am ten years older?' and 'Will I be able to do it with a problematic right knee?' This was an injury that kept getting better, but then would re-occur.

Injuries had never been a big problem for me in the past and I could normally ward off the little niggles, but this was proving to be persistent. Little did I know that one year later it would require major surgery?

A lifetime of fitness paid great dividends, but the real benefit was in my mental strength of being able to do the work and then switch off to run the business.

Knowing I had done this before was a great start: the ten years of training and running being a huge psychological advantage. What I was losing with age was more than made up with a decade of experience in covering the marathon and ultra distance events.

It is now nearly thirty years since the 50th and thinking back I can analyse how and why this mammoth task was achieved without any real fatigue or debilitation in the system. I remembered what my Dad used to tell me about his early days as a boxer.

He said, 'I used to get pasted, but gradually I learned how to hit and how not to get hit and then one day I learned how to fight.'

The how and why are simple: just keep doing it. Keep repeating what you have to do and the process will look after itself. In other words – the whole mind and body thing is about the three D's – doing – doggedness and determination – no bullshit – no rocket science – no problem.

TRAINING INTO OLD AGE

MEN DO NOT quit playing because they grow old – they grow old because they quit playing said Oliver Wendal Holmes.

Not that I remember playing at anything, I have enjoyed all or most of what I did.

It has taken me to the age of seventy-eight to admit I am old. The mind is still working, but the body less so. Still I am not yet finished.

When we were opening our Health Club in 1972, a sixty-year old called Bob Maunde came in and asked about 'this 'ere weight lifting.' Bob was a member for ten years and he even entered a couple of bodybuilding competitions.

My Dad trained until he was ninety. He swam every day and it was only bladder trouble and the fitting of a catheter that put an end to most of his activities, but he still carried on walking.

Bert Loveday, who I have mentioned in an earlier chapter, was still bench-pressing over 200lbs at the age of eighty-four. Malcolm Pittock, a local lad, is still running at the age of eighty-two. Ron Hill, an idol of mine, is now seventy-four and was placed twenty-third in an open running race climbing to over one thousand feet.

In Bill Pearl's book 'Getting Stronger,' he writes about Bob Anderson: Bob's best selling book 'Stretching' describes getting older as the 'creeping rigor mortis syndrome.'

As we get older we all slow down and stiffen up. In many cases this is a result of not keeping active. It is called sacropenia, a Latin

Photos of Bert Loveday at 23 – 50 – 80 years of age.

word meaning muscle waste. The best way of avoiding this is by keeping active. 'Life is Movement' was a book written by the Victorian Strongman Eugene Sandow, highly respected and courted by the Kings and Queens of his time. Sandow published many books on the virtues of exercise and pioneered his theories in schools, the armed forces, setting up health centres throughout Europe.

Biology, hereditary and moderate physical activity are the key issues to health and fitness in old age. We don't have too much control over the first two, although some have control over the latter. The choice of exercise is entirely up to the individual, but from someone who has been involved with so many variations of fitness, walking is hard to beat. There is no excuse for us not to do some form of physical activity in the latter part of our lives.

The one thing I have always advocated is consistency in any programme. Have a plan, the body responds to habit. If it is a walking programme make walking your habit, the same with the gym, the swim or the exercise class. Be consistent. Regularity will achieve results.

Another tip is to always keep within your limits. By all means be progressive, but slow and steady is the mantra. The old adage we used in running applies at any age: not too fast, not too hard, not too far, and remember this. This is your time, your life and your body.

Age and exercise in the twenty-first century do not hold the fear they did years ago. Activity programmes abound in Local Authority centres throughout the UK. Major Health Clubs are popular with the silver surfers. Fun runs seem to attract more and more of the grey population as fifty and sixty year olds are not even considered old. Choose your mode of exercise, join a health club or an activity centre or simply just go out and walk.

The Hardest Exercise of All

Slowing down is inevitable. Everything diminishes with age. The internal systems are no exception. The first signs are usually the pockets of weight around the middle on the glutes and thighs in women and the stomach in men. This is because the body's digestive systems are less efficient. This slowing down process then has its effect on the way the body burns energy with the unwanted calories turning to fat. This inevitably means we need less food.

The process starts at about fifty years of age with the rule of thumb guide being approximately one per cent per year. This equation means that by the time you are eighty you will have become thirty per cent less efficient. You can combat this by being more pro-active with your exercise. Switch your activities to more fat burning exercise and be conscious of not being inactive; keep moving and take a couple of short walks each day. There will also be a degree of muscle loss (sacrophenia), so use the exercise to keep up the muscle strength and tone. Most of all, face the fact that this will happen.

My advice is to eat less: the percentage of energy we lose should equate to a percentage of food, so by the time you reach sixty you will be eating ten per cent less and so on. The golden rule is honesty. Be straight, otherwise you will be fooling no one but yourself.

My Dad always said,

'The hardest exercise of all is to push yourself away from the table.' How right he was.

Is It All in the Mind?

Being overweight is not breaking any laws. I know lots of people who are carrying more than they should yet still remain active and healthy and in many cases live well into their seventies and eighties. But, all the studies and research shows we invite problems when carrying excess baggage. On the other hand, obesity is a non-negotiable. A stone or even two is to some degree acceptable, but not three!

Statistics show that a fifth of the British public is obese. In America this figure is as high as one in four. These figures are rising with each successive year with Britain now being the fattest country in Western Europe. Only Hungary has fatter people.

Most of the problems with weight and age are in the mind: you need an attitude of wanting to be better, fitter and healthier and do things in your daily life that are encouraging. Write down your eating plan and choose people you know with a similar lifestyle. Have a goal in mind, a timeline and believe consciously that you will get to where you want to be. Don't get over anxious when things are not going right. The simple advice is just stay positive.

Mental rehearsal is something athletes use constantly: this is about seeing what you want to look and feel like. Keep on looking for the new you. Keep that picture in your mind and to get the best out of yourself practise the imagery every day.

We are to some extent victims of our genes or what we inherited:

we are also what we think and what we do. Just believe in yourself and in doing so you will create habits that change your life.

I have just read a book over three hundred pages long on the latest diet and weight loss. It is a good book, but weight loss can be summed up in just three words 'Eat Less Food.' So between my Dad and those three wise words you can reach your desired weight. The old adage contains a lot of truth.

Bill Pearl is now in his eighty-fourth year: in a recent conversation I asked,

'Are you still working out?'

'Yes, Judy and I still train four days a week, but now we only do forty minutes.'

For most of his life Bill would train for two hours a day and much more when preparing for a competition.

My old friend Bert Loveday who lived to be ninety trained regularly and well into his late eighties. He could still lift 220 lbs in the Bench Press and was in fantastic shape until his final two years. Even well into his seventies Bert would play squash two or three times a week – a true example of regular exercise and the right mental approach – eighty-eight years of quality living.

Like my Dad, Bert lived through two world wars: a very restricted lifestyle, meagre rations, very little going for them and nothing like the benefits of today.

In my early running days, one of my first acquaintances was a man called Billy Leach. Billy was another who would run and walk well into his nineties. We both competed in the 1976 World Veteran Championships held in Coventry. I was forty-one and he was seventy. He completed the race in about 3 hrs.15 mins finishing in second place.

Billy, Bert and my Dad lived a life of frugal means. If you asked Billy about his diet he would quote his favourite dish of 'Pudding in Rag.' This was a dish of mince encased in suet pastry wrapped in a tea towel (rag) and boiled in a pan of simmering water.

'If thee's never had pudding in rag thee's never lived,' he would say.

A far cry from the obsessive life of today and the mountains of books telling us what to eat!

They were just three out of hundreds. People who were healthy, vibrant and full of life all living to a good age – a lesson for all of us.

The one tip I always advise is to never get wrapped up in the obsession of a diet. It is true; Billy and Dad's age had the restrictions of life to cope with. They ate less processed food and the simple fare only had a little extra salt added. They ate mostly what they could get fresh, meaning there was less need for preservatives – less sugar, less fat and no additives. All the cattle were fed the natural way: free range chickens producing free range eggs – no fish farms – a much simpler existence.

Working-out in Old Age

Cindy Crawford is one of the super models of our time along with Naomi Campbell, Twiggy, Chris Turlington and Linda Evangelista.

On commenting about her figure to Net à Porter Magazine, she opened up about her concerns with her weight.

'When nearing fifty I would love to lose about 5 lbs, but the cost means a gruelling regime: no salad dressing – no glass of wine – no fun.' Welcome to the real world and all because we slow down.

The nation as a whole is just getting fatter. A report by the Institute of Fiscal Studies highlights the problem of age, weight and fitness. We are now consuming less, but still put on the pounds: this is because we become more susceptible to sugar and fat. The average adult can cut calories by as many as six hundred a day, but because of our metabolic rate we still gain weight. It goes on to say we put on about half a pound a year. By the time you reach fifty you could weight thirty pounds more.

According to the report the slowing down process is due to changing eating habits, less exercise and just getting older with the sedentary life of modern day playing a huge part. There is no alternative – we either cut down or we put on weight.

My early inspiration Jack la Laine lived well into his nineties. He claimed to eat just two meals a day and like Miss Crawford he would come to terms with growing older, but unlike her, he would do without the salad cream and the wine.

It will help if you set goals and write them down so you know what you want and where you want to go. This will give you a measure of what you have and what you want to achieve. Keep this image in your mind.

Science has made huge progress in understanding how our mind works and it can help enormously by just keeping the thoughts at the forefront.

Society today imposes more pressures than ever before. We are subject to enormous mind games to eat, drink and buy all kinds of processed foods which are heavy in sugar, salt and fat. Rules, regulations and watchdog committees can only do so much; we have to do our share by taking responsibility. Goals and targets need not add to that pressure: it takes just a mental shift in the mind to encourage us to think differently on how we shop and take care of our input and the output of our energies.

Change is inevitable: after sixty-three years of weights, running and swimming, I have now opted for recreational swims with weights restricted to two days a week. Thankfully I can swim well and average in the region of about four miles per week. Eight years ago my right knee was replaced restricting me to the crawl, but somehow that is enough.

When old age beckons the quote by Charles Darwin 'It is not the strongest or the fastest that survive, but the ones who adapt' pretty much sums it up. We all have to find our level in accepting we are getting older and not make excuses to take it easy.

Follow the rules, adapt and if it is of any use here are my ten commandments for keeping active and being better in old age:

1.   Consistency: nothing worthwhile is achieved without it.
2.   Change: insanity is described as keep doing the same thing every day and expecting things to change, so make the changes.
3.   Don't be a victim: Heredity is not a reason, it's an excuse.
4.   Be inspirational: not to others but to yourself.
5.   Set goals and have targets.
6.   Sixty was old in the sixties. It's not old now, set the trend.
7.   Don't fool yourself: be honest.
8.   Keep your weight to an acceptable level.
9.   Be positive: rehearse the new you.
10.   Take time out to smell the roses.

DRUGS

THE USE OF anabolic steroids in gyms has now reached epidemic proportions. In gathering information for this chapter I have been into more than forty different clubs and gyms. I have met with owners, managers, users, dealers, policemen, medics, beginners and seasoned bodybuilders and on all occasions I have been met with honesty, frankness and even some disbelief at how quickly this problem has escalated.

This dramatic change in steroid abuse is predominantly down to three things. Firstly, the huge boom in superbly equipped budget clubs. These clubs have brought a new dimension to weight training and fitness with their large training areas and great equipment at budget prices of between £10 and £15 per month. The big chains and small independent operators are now being challenged as never before. This has caused a minor revolution in the gym business by attracting hard core bodybuilders to mix with young and very often naïve beginners. The budget clubs have huge memberships of four, five, six and even seven thousand members and provide an abundance of excellent training facilities. This mass input into training is bringing with it an exposure we have never seen before.

Secondly, it is now much easier to access these drugs. The stuff now comes in from China, Mexico, Manilla, Egypt or anywhere a manufacturer can be sourced: drugs that could have been made for use in animals or humans. The naïve, ignorant and sometimes the criminal are now the present day suppliers.

Third is the quite unexpected boost to the underworld economy from the fabricated world of showbiz. The instant gratification with made to measure pecs, abs and muscular biceps is the result of a ten week intensive course or courses of weight training and a cocktail of drugs that build up, strip down and fine tune the body, or should I say parts of the body that look good on our action heroes as seen by the young and vulnerable. The next time you see your cinematic idol baring his or her chest think 'Designer built – chemically enhanced.'

My first encounter with the magic pills was in 1972 when I flushed the first handful of Dianabol down the pan! My statement was clear then. No steroids, no drugs, but even then I knew that there would be no stopping it. Just not on my patch. I understand the need to

176

compete at a high level. Without artificial testosterone and the like there is no elite. Over the last forty years I have listened and understood the dilemma of top athletes, particularly bodybuilders. The main thing coming out of this research was finding out just how open the abuse is. It is in total contrast to the principles of athletics and sport.

Bodybuilding and fitness is a multi-million pound business employing fifty-sixty thousand people – a huge contribution to the economy. Yet, there is little legislation to make the clubs safe places for kids to go. There is a lack of knowledge and education. Personal trainers, managers and reception workers all come into contact with the customer – with the use of drugs being rampant on the gym floor.

Dianabol was first used 1950 in the Soviet Union, according to Ivan Waddington and Andy Smith. It was discovered by Dr John Zeigler, the physician for the American athletic team. In their book 'Drugs in Sport', Smith and Waddington acknowledged that Zeigler returned to the States and introduced drugs to Bob Hoffman who at the time was the USA weightlifting coach. Hoffman was not one for missing a trick and introduced them to his team – the rest is history! It should be said, however, that anabolic steroids were not then a banned substance, with the use of manufactured testosterone still an unknown quantity. The long-term effects were not yet known, but there was no shortage of athletes ready to enhance their performance. Dianabol has now been around for over sixty years: taken in moderation and prescribed by a doctor and for the right reason it will do more good than bad, but when taken at more than ten times the recommended dosage it can have devastating results.

In his three books 'Giants of the Weight Game' Bill Pearl also acknowledges Zeigler's contribution to the present day dilemma. Pearl, who is as close to the bodybuilding scene as anyone can get, says in his book Zeigler confessed on his death-bed saying he wished he had never discovered the muscle-building drugs. Zeigler thought the drugs had brought on the heart condition of which he subsequently died.

In the last fifty years there have been thousands of reports of the misuse of steroids. Heart disease, kidney, liver, prostate damage, testicular cancer and death have all been related to the overuse of bodybuilding drugs. Half a century ago, had it not been Zeigler it would have been someone else starting the greed that is now morphing itself into a horror story of unimaginable magnitude.

The Frankenstein Syndrome

If there is a way to create an advantage, we will take it. I can honestly say, with hand on heart, if the stuff had been around when I was in my teens I would have seriously considered it. The young people of today are just like I was in those early years: working like hell, buying the bodybuilding magazines, talking shop with my peers and desperately trying to keep up appearances. In today's world I would have been tempted and found it more difficult to resist the opportunity, if it had been widely known that my film idol was building his body with the help of a few pills. The pictures in the magazines were examples of what I wanted and if my colleagues in the gyms had the means…?

The science of it all is now right here and readily available and there is not a gym in the country that is not beleaguered by this problem.

'The kids come to me for a bodybuilding programme and ask me to supply them with steroids' says a highly respected physiotherapist with a great set-up, a well equipped gym, one of the most knowledgeable people known both as a physio and bodybuilder. He also knows in depth about nutrition and has an in-depth understanding of steroids and the associated drugs.

He, like me, knows there are no instant results.

'Kids of sixteen and seventeen come and ask for the gear as though they are asking for vitamin tablets or protein powder. They even know about stacking or cocktailing – terms used for using three or four different kinds of drugs at the same time. They seem to think that this is all they need. I don't sell stuff; I sell protein, vitamin and mineral supplements. They don't realise that it takes years to build a good physique.'

There are now drugs to 'build up', drugs to 'strip off the fat', drugs to 'hide the drugs' in the system. The kids read about them, talk to the dealers about them and discuss it among their peers. My physio would go on to say

'Their ignorance of the effects is only because it is a buyer's market – a market that is saturated with gullible young people.'

Cocktailing or Stacking, using three or four of twenty or thirty available drugs, is being used without any real supervision: an ex-bodybuilder and pusher told me that some are using a mixture of recreational drugs in addition to the bodybuilding stuff. In some of the gyms it's like a scene from Alcatraz – testosterone driven to the point of overkill. There is a drug called Synthol that the kids are injecting. They can put two inches onto their arms in two days – the same is said of certain vegetable oils. Injecting directly into the muscle area gives instant and short term results; the names of testosterone, androgens, sustanon and winstrol all roll off the tongue of these young men who are not even bodybuilders, but are caught up in the frenzy of instant results, blind and limited to the facts that muscle is built over time and that, without the right genes, the gains will be limited.

The imports from Turkey, Egypt but mostly China, pushed through our clubs leave little room for negotiation or curtailment: this stuff is here and has been for years. We cannot beat it. The culture of drugs is now part of life. What we have to do is push for legislation, for some measure of education and control. Unless we have a measure of containment, we will never have a means to manage the problem.

When I talked with the dealers and users I got the distinct impression they wanted to talk. Perhaps they too are fed up with the hypocrisy. They know, like all the people on the inside, that this is not just about the kids, but the stars on the screen, in popular music and at the top of the athletic tree.

There has been more than one occasion when well known names in the world of sport have talked about a campaign for drug-free sport. Yes, she is taking EPO – he is on Sustanon or Enanthabe. On asking how they knew, the answer was 'I know the supplier.' When I asked about the side effects, the words testicular cancer always came up.

One said: 'By the time they reach the age of twenty-five these kids will be impotent.' They will have prostate problems or even cancer by the time they are twenty-five or thirty.

Our second most common cancer, prostate cancer is frequently mentioned along with kidney, liver, spleen and pancreatic – all part of the conversation. A reality? I do not know, but it is clearly a huge concern.

It is a lifetime away from when I flushed that first handful of Dianabol down the drain and it is over thirty years since Bill Pearl warned us about the overuse of steroids in his book 'Keys to the Inner Universe.'

In Chris Cooper's book 'Run, Swim, Throw, Cheat' he writes of catching the cheats, but how can they be cheating if everyone is using?

Are the kids naïve or is it political pressure?

There is no naivety in the gyms or fitness centres except for the affects: using drugs is now a fact of life and a disease of society. But who cares? It is just the future generation that is at risk and, of course, that is the truth.

There are three things we can do to manage this situation. First would be to appoint a controlling body to devote time and money to the problem. This could be the Industry Lead Body or the Sports Council. It could even be the Fitness Industry Association, Department of Trade and Industry, Customs and Excise or the Department of Media Culture and Sport. Who knows? It is a decision for the government.

Secondly, would be the action to educate the mums and dads of the kids. This could even start in the schools.

Thirdly, legislate for conditions that make the owners of all gyms big and small responsible for the people that use them.

The book 'Death in the Locker Room' written in the early 80's quotes the author Bob Goldman saying how the case of drugs had become epidemic with athletes. This epidemic has multiplied way beyond sport and elitism. It is eating away at our society, our homes, schools, gyms and youth of this country. It needs to stop, or at the very least, it needs managing.

The obvious start would be the instructors who need to gain a qualification for work. There is not one syllabus on any of the NVQ 1, 2 or 3 programmes that educates the workforce on the danger signs or how and why drugs work. Perhaps this is the starting point in helping to put some measure of control in our health clubs and gyms, as the effects of not taking action could be a generation of mutants with deformities. Be it communication, education or legislation – the answer is there – we just need to process it.

STEROID USE – THE PITFALLS

THE USE OF steroids will only work for a limited period of six to eight weeks. After this time the body's mechanism will shut down and the steroids will stop working. It is just like taking antibiotics with the body becoming immune. But the human psyche argues and the athlete stays on them hoping for more. He or she may continue to grow and if that is the case it is always due to the continuity of training.

Drugs alone will not get results: they do not work in any shape or form without hard training and good nutrition. It is like saying I can play an instrument better by taking a pill or play soccer better by having drugs. It Is nonsense to even think that results will happen without the dedication.

Talent and ability is a product of our genes: we either have it or we don't have it. The ability to be a Mr Universe or a Mr Britain is about hard work over time. It is called the ten thousand hour rule and a guide for people utilising their capacity for achievement and competence. Musicians, footballers, hockey players, lifters and bodybuilders spend years and thousands of hours working at their innate talent before reaching their true potential. This ten thousand hour rule is a guide used worldwide on what it takes to be the best you can be in the course of your training and your life.

Steroids are a chemical substance of the body's natural production of testosterone: testosterone regulates the reproductive cells that produce sperm in men. The overuse and over activity of this will cause the breakdown of the gland called the prostate. Prostate cancer is the second biggest killer in the world in men. But, both men and women can be affected by the use of steroids.

There are many young athletes, male and female, who risk impotency, liver and kidney failure, prostate cancer and other organ failures through overuse of artificial substances. These drugs should only be used on the recommendation of a doctor or physician, with the right dosage over a recommended period of time. The risk is too great with anything else.

Seven out of every ten men will have prostate trouble before they reach the age of seventy. Athletes overdosing on steroids could have this problem by their late twenties and thirties – add to that impotency and testicular cancer! It is a no brainer.

CASE STUDY – STEROID FEVER

THE BOY WAS twenty years of age and a junior bodybuilding champion: a product of a carefully thought-out hard, demanding weight programme covering every single body part to the smallest degree.

His nutrition programme consisted of six small meals per day timed to blend in with his weight programme and balanced to get the very best out of his obvious potential.

The third component of this young man's ambitious training schedule was a cocktail of steroids designed to work alongside his nutrients and weights.

On a Monday and Wednesday there would be 250 mgs of testosterone; on Friday trembolone acetate enanthate – a slow release drug that synthesizes more protein. This drug also creates oestrogen, a natural hormone in women. With men this will have the effect of forming fluid in the breast, resulting in something called 'bitch tits.' Another drug is then used to eliminate the side effects of brenbolone. In addition he also takes clenbuterol – a drug that opens the airways – a proven fat burner that can give you the shakes. This increases the metabolism and helps to burn fat, but it can also create asthma. Another drug called T3 increases the use of the thyroid and over a two month period will have the effect of shutting down the thyroid function. Somatropin is a hormone causing growth in areas not related to muscle building – enlarged feet, wrists and heart – a clear case of steroid fever and huge physical problems in the not too distant future.

The boy from Cheshire told me he does not plateau!

'I inject in the glutes and the fatty tissue at the side of the waist and in addition I also take 240 mgs of sustanon, this is used to promote weight gain, strength and the maintenance of muscle.'

This young man is on this stuff on an ongoing basis: six or seven drugs non-stop. His physique is beautiful, proportioned, ripped and his skin tone almost translucent. He looks the picture of health and well being and is the envy of many other young men in the gym, but he, just like thousands of others, sells to the willing buyer – all catching the fever of steroid use.

MOTIVATION

FOR A NUMBER of years I watched and supported two of my grand-children playing football: Joe and Matthew were eighteen months apart in age, so that meant two games each week. Joe was a goalie and struggled because of his size, but with perseverance and determination he became a good goalie. Matt, on the other hand was a talented player who flourished. He was fast on the ball, had good eye, hand and foot co-ordination.

For six years Saturday morning was a non-negotiable, always dominated by football with the lads playing for different clubs. Matt played for Turton Tigers, a local team that gradually over time became the one to watch. After completing ten years as manager, Julian Bancroft decided to retire. The lads were getting older, less controllable and starting to lose interest. Julian in his wisdom had already picked his successor and suddenly I found myself in charge of eighteen young lads who were biologically on the verge of manhood.

At the age of 73 I was not overly convinced that I wanted any kind of management and was somewhat reluctant. I knew nothing about managing a soccer team. I had no qualifications, no idea of tactics, passages of play, team selection or even the much bigger picture of organising soccer pitches and league administration. Three words summed it up – I knew nowt!

The Tigers was just one of sixteen teams playing for Turton Football Club: subscriptions, training grounds, kit, practise nights, fixture lists, and parents' involvement, all added to the responsibility. None of this would faze me: the challenge was the thought of how an ageing grandfather with an age difference of over fifty years and without an ounce of credibility could motivate these young men to follow his example.

Turton FC is one of the oldest football clubs in the world: Bolton Wanderers and the football league evolved from it more than one hundred years ago. The main ground is surrounded by exquisite countryside, perched high above the Wayoh Reservoir. It is an area blessed with rolling hills, wooded landscape, rivers, streams and green fields rich with wildlife. This pocket of paradise winds its way down from the Darwen Moor and Broadhead Valley and is the result of having meandered from the Trough of Bowland and the Ribble Valley some twenty miles to the north.

The training ground of Turton Tigers however, is to the west of this small fissure of beauty and not quite as idyllic. It sits on the edge of the moor of gorse and course grass, a pitch that rocks more than it rolls. It is undersized, windswept and affords little protection from the north winds. It has a windowless chicken coop that serves as a storeroom for old dilapidated lawn mowers, ancient grass rollers, a home to stray pigeons and also a changing room and shelter for the teams. It was here in this aberration of elite football I conducted my first ever motivational talk to my squad of fifteen year old soccer players.

The team's performance over the past three seasons had been quite moderate: mid table, maybe a hundred goals conceded with ninety goals scored. One week they would win a game 7 – 0 and the next lose by the same score. In truth, they were like any other team throughout the country with scouts cherry-picking the talent and filtering it out to the more professional clubs. Although I had no managerial experience in soccer, what I did have was over forty years of managing teams of people in business. Applying this experience to a group of lads shouldn't have really been a problem, but crucially, the one thing I needed from them was an element of belief. This single ingredient is the one thing that all motivation is dependent on and my

From moderation to excellence.

tenure as a football manager without this belief would simply not get off the ground. I needed to earn their trust.

These lads would not understand my background or my history and probably had little knowledge of the Second World War, let alone what I had done in business, so it was important for me to set the whole of the season in motion with a talk of some importance. If this was going to work it had to start with a vote of confidence. What I said to them on that first training session on that windswept hill went something like this.

OK lads, let's have you in, I want to ask you some questions. I want you to think back over the past two seasons and ask yourselves how well you performed. I don't want you to tell me now, just hold the answers in your mind. You all know where you finished in the league last season and the season before, but what I want to know is how you are going to perform this season. (I'll explain)

'You finished half-way up the league. Are you going to do the same again or are you going to finish three places above or below that position? Are you going to finish three places from the top or do you believe you can do better? I want you to see that position in your mind and hold it there.

'This season you are going to train harder than you have ever trained before. We now have a coach and we are going to concede fewer goals, be more organised and play better football. We are a team: the team is the squad; the squad is you, your fellow players, your parents and the people who come to support you. I have six conditions.

1.   We enjoy our football
2.   We believe we can win every game
3.   We respect our opponents
4.   We pull for one another
5.   We fight for every ball, every square foot of the pitch, every blade of grass
6.   We show respect and we demand respect

The lads went on to win every match bar one in the league, winning by eight clear points and reducing their deficit of goals by 30%. They were also runners up in the cup final. The following year they won the league again – so back to back promotions. In those two seasons we only recruited three players, with all but one living in the immediate area of Turton.

There has never been any doubt in my mind when taking on the mantle of leadership for any group of people, you must first get them to see what the summit looks like and the end result before the journey starts.

Our journey started on the hills above Bolton: a ramshackle collection of mediocrity, a mid-table team, a joke of a pitch, a bunch of hormone-driven kids without direction, goals or ambitions and probably the most important thing of all, a shoulder to lean on when navigating along the treacherous path to the top. Motivation is not about doing; it's about getting others to do it and giving the direction.

Whilst writing this I went out to speak to one of the player's parents. Someone I rarely see these days. Graham Brushett is the Dad of Sam, my centre back who was big and strong and as I was about to discover later, courageous and tough when needed. I still have a picture in my mind of Sam in the penalty box, bloodied after a clash of heads, during a melee of arms, legs, heads and bodies with feelings running high. Sam was out to the world, but valiantly came back on the pitch which helped us to eventually win the match on penalties. Sam's attitude to the game was consistent with every single player of that squad and me going out to Graham was literally just a stab in the dark.

'Write me one line' I asked him, 'just one line that expresses your thoughts as a parent on your time with Turton Tigers. He did not write one line he wrote a whole page and this is what he had to say.

Ken Heathcote – moulding success with Turton Tigers

Ken took over a group of young players that had been together since the age of eight and who lived in and around the Edgworth and Turton area. The squad had a diverse range of talent, but they had come together as friends from the same school. Enjoyment was the common denominator – they wanted to kick a ball most Saturday mornings on the off chance that the occasional game would see them win, even though their parents had higher expectations!

Ken stepped in and the whole ethos changed. He supervised regular training and coaching sessions in a manner that demanded commitment and discipline. Ken commanded respect and the players gained more self-respect from playing in a more organised and consistent manner. The players flourished under the guidance of a young coach that was brought by Ken to motivate the boys during training. In the past the team relied

on the goodwill of parents to bring the best out of the boys. But this was not enough. Ken was determined that the boys should maximise their potential as people as well as players.

Ken laid out precisely what he expected in terms of personal strengths and attitudes at all times. If any of the players did not fulfil his expectations they were given a chance to improve or they were out. In this sense he was strict, but he was also impartial and fair. The players knew exactly where they stood and respected his even-handed approach, even though it was tough for them to take on occasions.

The old adage is that 'success breeds success.' This was certainly true under Ken's leadership. The team were virtually unbeaten under his management in the league competitions and they achieved great results in the cup competitions against sides that were performing in higher leagues. Much of this success is down to Ken, whose energy and determination were much admired by the parents who supported their boys in what became a very accomplished side capable of playing flowing and attractive football. He became a fine role model not just for the players whom he nurtured, but also to the adults who valued his tremendous energy and authority.

Graham's letter says it all: ethos, consistency, discipline, reciprocal respect, organisation, attitudes and the maximization of what we had with our players. Motivation is no more, no less, than the sum of all these things. It was a privilege to work with those boys and a privilege to work with their parents.

The Psychology

Not many people will believe that a four minute speech on a windswept pitch on the moors above Bolton won the lads two successive league titles in two years. Motivation is a mixture, a blend of values and beliefs and a strict set of rules to work to. Words are never enough, but very often they can be the starting point to a campaign like I had with the lads. They can also be a programme of exercises to change your life.

There are thousands of stories on how teachers have motivated pupils to excel in schools, not so much by their words, but how they resonated with them. Their attitude, body language and how they articulated the message. It is the same with a sports coach and a trainer:

some can squeeze the best out of people by not what they say but by how they say it. There is only about 7% of a speech remembered; the remaining 93% is remembered on how it is said and through the non-verbal language of the body. The psychology of motivation is a combination of all these things, but it will always start with trust.

Winning the hearts and minds of people effectively starts with us. We need to understand how people think and receive information. A good motivator will understand what another person wants, why they want it, how to communicate it and when to press the button or throw the switch. Life works in a linear way. We think about things, we talk about what we thought and then act on what we have talked about. These three things shape our habits and it's the habits that shape our character and define our destiny.

Think, talk, act, habit, character, and destiny: these six steps are the subconscious working on automatic pilot. We all do it: some people will go through their life doing nothing else. To change, we need to change that linear way of thinking and by doing that we change the habit. Then, if we are to be successful the habit needs to be a better habit than we had in the past.

The changes to the lads' football habits were minimal, just one extra night's training each week with punctuality a non-negotiable, but the shift in their mental attitude was enormous: As treats we had pasta evenings, pie and peas and curry nights. We bought black travelling tops to match the socks and shorts of their kit; this presented a more formidable uniform when arriving for a game. Looking smart, organised, disciplined and arriving early ready to go through the pre-game drills helped forge a mentality of togetherness and was all a part of the presentation, giving the opponents, who arrived in twos and threes, something to think about and take notice. In business this is called culture: for our lads, a change in football DNA – new ways, new habits, new team.

Inspire

Inspiring is that divine influence that comes first but is short lived: motivation is constant and carries us forward. When I went out to train with Steve Kenyon and Deeks Costella I was inspired for weeks. I was inspired by their presence, their company and their status. That flush of inspiration was like a bolt of electricity, as was the talk on the moors.

When researching this book and talking to Stuart Cosgrove, he recalled the visits in the seventies of all the champion bodybuilders and Mr Universe winners who had visited our club.

Stuart said, 'When I was in my twenties I trained with Bill Pearl who was then in his fifties and on one occasion I remember we had three Mr Britain winners training with him because they just wanted to be in his presence. Pearl's greatness was in his ability to accommodate everyone and everything in his company. The workouts were hard and demanding and at the same time conversational, reciprocal and adaptive.

Pearl would say, 'You pick the next exercise Stuart and then I will pick the one after that', and this would go on throughout the two and a half hour training session.

Everyone would be inspired by the easy attitude of Bill while working out with these young guns; they were training with a man considered by many to be the best ever. The only man to get under the skin of Schwarzenegger!

If used correctly, inspiration is the catalyst of change. When Gerry Luczka asked me to do my charity muscle marathon (his words, not mine) for the people of the Johnson Fold Estate he used the word catalyst. It proved to be the right thing at the right time to change the whole dynamics of the campaign.

By winning six squash world championships Jonah Barrington inspired a whole nation by stepping into a squash court to play a game that only a few years previously was obsolete and had been a mystery to all. Seb Coe's 2012 Olympic Games, Andy Murray's win at Wimbledon in 2013 and Baby George, the son of the Duke and Duchess of Cambridge inspired millions. Inspiration moves us, shakes us, stirs our blood, lifts our spirits and stimulates the heart and the mind.

Aspire

The sports day at Kearsley Wear Junior School was held in the playground: coconut matting was strewn across concrete surfaces with chalk-lines representing the start for the fifty-yard dash. A tape or piece of string held by two pupils was the finishing line. One of the mats served as a sandpit for the long jump – it was not the breeding ground for future Olympians. It was sport languishing at the foot of the curriculum ladder; no questions asked, just a break from the three R's and other subjects that thwarted our creative ability.

The sports day was a welcome adventure: for me, running, jumping or any of the activities was a means of expression. Even at the tender age of eight I was competitive, without being particularly good. There was not even a hint of the life that would follow; it was just a reward in itself. But on looking back was there something of the aspirations for the future?

I remember that day and how I was carried away by the sheer exuberance of just being out of the classroom. In the warm up, if you could call it that, I was running and jumping better than the rest, but when it came to the real thing I was left trailing at the back, but, instead of being fazed, the opposite happened.

Many years later I stood in front of thousands of young people who all wanted to aspire to work in the fitness industry: people, who in most cases were at the bottom end of the food chain in terms of prospects or opportunities. I know, because I had been one of them many times. I started with my successive string of failures and through perseverance became the darling of the health club scene. Our training courses were a good platform in helping a part of our nation to aspire to be better. If there is a message to come out of this chapter it is that failure is only failure if it stops or ends your dreams. Regardless of your talent, prospects or opportunities, failure is just a part of success when aspiring to be better. Trust me, I know, I have been there.

HOW IT ALL BEGAN – FAMILY – PRICELESS

It's now or never that you will be – It's now or never...

IT WAS 1956 and Elvis Presley was No 1 in the charts when during the interval at the Bolton Palais de Dance in 1956 I first acknowledged this young seventeen year old called Brenda Walsh. We had met briefly six days before whilst doing a demonstration of exercises organised by Cab Cashford at the Co-op Weight Training Club.

The twelve girls in their white tops and blue knickers had given a display of a version of exercise to music along with eleven lads flexing their muscles for the audience.

Now a few days later and with very little recollection of our brief meeting this young blonde, who with the merest provocative flick of her head, imperceptible eye contact and the hint of a smile would capture me for ever and all time. The words of Elvis – 'Come here my darling, hold me tight – kiss me my darling, your mine tonight' would stay in my memory to this day. The night was young and we were young: the age of music would throb to the beat of rock and roll and

Dining out with my Mum Norah and Dad Joe.

the smooch as only the young can do. Ignore convention, protocol, introduction, dialogue and act with abandonment of everything that is sensible – pledge a life together.

Our livelihoods limited us to a few bob for the latest vinyl record, a pair of blue suede shoes or a made to measure suit from Burtons: the Sunday treat was hanging out at the ice cream parlour of Sabini's, Morelli's and Tognarelli's for the latest American cream soda, hot vimto, sarsaparilla or milk shake. The Cappuccino would later become the rage in the coffee bars and venues of the Beatles. The revolution of rock, pop and skiffle and a fusion to accommodate an explosion of sounds as the lyric took second place to the interpretation of music.

Like all young people we would go with a click! Ours being hell bent on weights. The bodybuilding era, before the musclemen would grace our cinema and TV screens, was still two decades away, and before the age of steroids. It was before the likes of Stallone and Schwarzenegger, and the bulging pecs and six packs that now frequent our screens of today.

Our scene was made up of Malcolm (Doc) Doran – Pat and Mike

Paul with his sister Karen and her husband Ian.

192

McCarthy – Big Pete McDermott – Keith (Willy) Williamson – Roy Keats – Tommy Temperley and the older generation of Bert (Mr Britain) Loveday – Cab Cashford – and jumping Jim Halliday.

The Aspins – Nibbletts – Big Jim Foy – Bert Owen – BoBo Matu and the Royal Brothers would embrace the sport of Amateur and Professional Wrestling. They would win us medals and fill the small screens with Jackie Pallo – Big Bill Benny – Haystacks Calhoun – Big Daddy – and Mick McManus.

On the female side we would gaze at our own girls – June Wall – Brenda Walsh – Dorothy Kay – Renee Price with graceful figures, lifting heavy weights, tearing telephone directories in half and bending six inch nails – beauties and beasts – strength and grace – youth and maturity – all packaged in the youth of the day. A rich time that was full of energy, love and life.

Brenda and I would marry on the 5th September 1959 at St Peters Church in Farnworth and with no limits to our imagination and abandonment of money hold the reception at the Clock Face Pub just a few yards from my childhood home. But we did have champagne! Her Dad Arthur had bought six bottles of Moet Chandon. Before the night was out we would head to the Black Horse Pub where we boarded a Yellow-Ways Coach transporting us to Newquay for our honeymoon. Romance had no limits – we would spend our first night together on a bus – a thirteen hour journey to Cornwall. The last of the big time Charlies, that's us! No limits to expense, imagination and romantic endeavour.

The summer of '59 was a splendid year with a heat-wave lasting through to October. The Beachcroft Hotel offered panoramic views across the Atlantic Ocean: bed/breakfast/lunch/evening meals/entertainment and a wonderful service for the princely sum of 11 guineas per week. We had before us some of the most stunning coastline in the world with beautiful beaches and surf: a coastline that would attract millions in the future.

This rather low-key romantic launch of a lifetime together gave no indication of the future: a partnership that at the time had little promise other than two kids. We were starting out on a journey like millions of others throughout the world, but would, in time, reap a life of some vintage.

Paul was born on the 3rd October 1960 and Karen, some seventeen months later. They would both enter this world in the front bedroom of our home in Kildare Street, Farnworth. For all its modesty and lowly status Farnworth did have a better area with a few streets of houses built in Accrington Bricks – not posh – just a bit nicer. The two up, two down with an outside toilet and a bathroom the size of a cupboard would be our home for the next decade. Dr John Gracie, an individual of rare quality would deliver both our children and solicit my help on these occasions. As was his habit, our good Doctor would celebrate with a wee dram of whisky – a habit we would share for the next ten years. Never ever showing reluctance our Scottish Physician would treat us and our children with a casual respect and an amiable disposition with anything from chicken pox to wind – midwifery duties to measles – a generation of ordinary people sharing the challenges of everyday ordinary things in life.

Throughout the sixties I would continue to run the club in the cellar at Chancery Lane. In those early days we had no car, so to run the gym I travelled each night into Bolton by bus, week in and week out. I would also look for extra work to boost my meagre wages of bricklaying.

Our first ten years of marriage was a mixture of idiosyncrasies with the building trade being subject to many changes: sometimes it offered good wages, but in bad weather it offered no wages! I would

Our four grandchildren at the Longridge Restaurant.

take work wherever I could get it. I would do some modelling at the Art College and also take up Professional Wrestling for about two years. With no car I had to rely on my Dad for transport to the venues and work all this around a full-time job.

Wrestling at the same venues and sharing the car expenses was a friend of mine Roy Keats: he would wrestle under the name of Young Hackenschmit and I would be billed as Ken Zeldts (Who the hell thought of that name? but it stuck with me for a few years.) We wrestled mainly in clubs of the North West, Whitchurch, Manchester, Southport and Wrexham, where I was billed as undefeated in the country (Wales) – this was the absolute truth as I had never wrestled in Wales.

Wrestling was good fun but hard work: travelling to venues and having to perform in some night club or old cinema with no changing room or shower was challenging. The best you could expect was a bucket to wash in! Not glamorous in any way and if you were lucky you would finish up with a tenner for your trouble.

Wrestling, modelling, running a gym and bricklaying was not the

Paul, Sam, Georgia and Gabbi in the courtyard at Buckingham Palace after Paul had received his MBE.

ideal way to bring up two children, but at the time it was all we had. I suppose you could call it a time of discovery! But there must have been some instinct buried deeply that was searching for something to provide us with a good livelihood. Gut instinct was telling me there was something better – but what?

Brenda did know there was something better! In the mid-sixties we had bought our first car – a car I had purchased in the evening dusk and to find out the following morning it was the paint that was holding it together. However, the Morris Minor did serve its purpose and to some degree was a step in the right direction.

The winter of 1967 was bad for the building trade with both Bill and I having a spell at working at Chloride Batteries in an attempt to earn a regular income. Neither of us was suited to factory work and we made the decision to have a go at working for ourselves. Becoming self-employed seemed to set a precedent for the future.

With our grandsons Matthew and Joe at the National Fitness Awards 2011 after receiving my third Lifetime Achievement Award.

We undertook work building extensions, putting in new windows and replacing gutters. In fact we built the occasional house. We would turn our hands to anything that earned us a crust! Somehow we managed to earn enough to support our families.

When I came up with the idea of moving from Chancery Lane to Bank Street it seemed a logical thing to do. It was an extension of our building partnership and a business move of necessity if we wanted to grow.

In the meantime Paul and Karen were growing up. Brenda was having designs on moving to a better house in a better district. I wasn't sure how you could beat a house built of Accrington brick, but with my limited vision on domestic matters I would be led by her judgement. What was not apparent but lurking beneath the surface was the feeling that something was about to change – that change was Mawdsley Street and with the change would come a change of mentality. From being a brickie, a battery assembler, odd job man, wrestler and model I now had a vision, a mission and a passion – I now wanted the best gym in the country.

At the time I was subscribing to an American magazine called 'Iron Man' and happened to read an article written by a guy called Arthur Jones about a new idea he was floating. He was marketing pieces of equipment he called 'Cam Operated Variable Resistance Machines' – a new concept in training and for some unknown reason I saw this as a kind of omen. It was not so much about the equipment, but the way he spoke and marketed the concept – it was innovative and full of promise.

All of this was floating in and out of my mind whilst dealing with a potential house change, a gym to be moved, children growing up, trying to make a living, and strange as it may seem, trying to keep in shape as well.

The move from Chancery Lane to Bank Street followed by the move to Mawdsley Street coincided with the maturity of our children and relocation to greener pastures.

Turton High School and Eagley Junior School would be a transition for Paul and Karen. A transition in culture, a different way of thinking and a lifestyle removed from the cobbled streets of Farnworth and outside toilets. The insistence of Brenda for us to move was probably more productive in terms of change than our move across town to Mawdsley Street. It was not about status or the standard of living. It was not about a better education or so called trappings of success. It was a simple matter of being better with a better home in a better area, better prospects for all of us.

Mum and Dad would also move from Farnworth to Turton. It was Brenda who once again spotted the opportunity to buy a cottage in need of repair and renovation. A bargain well within the financial reach of our parents and renovated by Bill and myself.

Unfortunately, Paul and Karen were taking after their Dad in not inheriting any real academic skills, but Paul's creative talents would draw him towards commercial art or the world of cooking. Fortunately for him he chose the latter and Karen would embark on a career in beauty therapy. Later in life, they would both expand their innovative talents and skills to diversify into other things.

Paul would develop his business skills and innovative talents to more corporate ventures whilst Karen would develop her management talents to co-run her husband's engineering businesses.

The turning point from Kildare Street to Haydock Lane was just a matter of six miles, but in terms of mentality, a giant leap of faith.

There would be no limits to what we could do now! The small back street black iron gym that had been so much a part of our lives and the move to our new home signalled a shift in thinking with the thinking turning to a more fulfilling life for all of us.

For Book signings – Seminars – Workshops

or a Ken Heathcote Masterclass contact us on

www.kenheathcote.co.uk/book

The start of the cycle.

Mrs Heathcote gets a round of applause from the players at Burnden Park

Grandma Heathcote's passion for Bolton Wanderers.

The continuation.

EPILOGUE

GRANDMA HEATHCOTE WAS an avid and passionate supporter of Bolton Wanderers and had a season ticket in the Wing Stand of the old Burnden Park. She would take me to the matches and I marvelled in her ability to see the game with such clarity and detail, particularly when play was at the far corner of the ground. It took me years to figure out that her unrestricted vocal support was only in evidence when a white shirt went down or was punished for some misdemeanour of the rules.

Years later, our son Paul also benefited from his great grandma's company and expertise of partisan and biased football. Just like me, he also valued the time spent sharing a common interest. We also both enjoyed the day seeing her exiting the players tunnel with Nat Lofthouse when she celebrated her 80th birthday and the players' clapping her out. I think she would have been particularly pleased that Nat arranged for the team to train on the weights at Bolton Health Studio forging a twenty year relationship with the club.

Burnden Park and Bolton Health Studio no longer exist but both institutions are remembered by many for providing an escape from the ordinary day to day things in life to bring pleasure, and in our case, hope and benefits of better health, well being and often a whole new life. The memories still flourish, the link to the past is over, but the future still holds promise of a further prolonged relationship.

It was announced on the 31st July that Paul's company, Heathcote & Co, would join Bolton Wanderers and the newly named Bolton Whites Hotel would benefit from the two star Michelin chef's expertise when taking over the catering for the stadium and hotel.

I think Grandma Heathcote would be proud of her name, her grandson's link with training the team and now her great-grandson's involvement with the hotel and stadium. A continuation of a tradition that has links with the past and has now forged another link to the future.

No doubt Paul and Gabbi's children, Georgia and Sam, will also enjoy some time at the Reebok along with Karen and Ian's boys, Joseph and Matthew. I hope they will all remember their roots, Burnden Park, Bank Street and Grandma Heathcote.

PROGRAMMES FOR MARATHON RUNNING

OVER A THIRTY year period we trained literally hundreds of people who were intent on running the marathon with most of them succeeding. The failure of the ones who did not succeed was always due to not following the mantra of 'not too fast – not too long – not too hard.' The early stages are crucial. Beginners should take a year to prepare, but I know only a few abide by these simple rules.

The thumb-rule guide to just get round is to cover the equivalent distance of 26 miles each week. The more you do above that will help you achieve the distance better and hopefully faster.

The following 2 programmes will help you negotiate the distance safely, progressively and competently.

The first programme is for a duration of 12 weeks and will help you build a resilience into the legs – don't underestimate how important this is.

The second programme will progress you to running a competent marathon that is more than a jog or just getting round. It is important you develop a consistency; time – rhythm – pace and consistency are the keys – not just in running, but in every sport and even in life.

THE YEAR AHEAD FOR THE COMPLETE BEGINNER

Week 1	2 runs of 1 mile each of easy running leave at least 2 days between runs	2.0 miles
Week 2	3 runs of 1 mile each of easy running on alternate days	3.0 miles
Week 3	3 runs of 1.2 miles easy running on alternate days	3.6 miles
Week 4:	3 runs of 1.5 miles easy running on alternate days	4.5 miles
Week 5	3 runs of 2 miles easy running each day	6.0 miles
Week 6	3 runs of 2.5 miles easy runs each day	7.5 miles
Week 7	3 runs of 3 miles easy running plus 1 more run of 2.5 miles	11.5 miles
Week 8	3 runs of 3 miles easy running plus 1 run of 4 miles	13.0 miles
Week 9	3 runs of 3 miles easy running plus 1 run of 5 miles	14.0 miles
Week 10	3 runs of 3 miles easy running plus 1 run of 6.5 miles	15.5 miles

Week 11	3 runs of 3 miles easy running. Plus 1 run of 6.5 miles	15.5 miles
Week 12	3 runs of 3 miles easy running. Plus 1 run of 6.5 miles	15.5 miles

This very moderate and slow start will not make you into a running star, but it will prepare the essential muscle joints and tendons. It will also prepare you for the discipline – the most important of all the essentials.

12 WEEK COURSE

Week	Days	Total
Week 1	Monday 6 miles Tuesday 6 miles Wednesday 10 miles Thursday 3 miles Friday 3 miles Saturday (Rest) Sunday 12 miles	40
Week 2	Monday 4 miles Tuesday 7 miles Wednesday 10 miles Thursday 4 miles Friday 7 miles Saturday (Rest) Sunday 13 miles	45
Week 3	Monday 4 miles Tuesday 8 miles Wednesday 10 miles Thursday 4 Miles Friday 8 miles Saturday (Rest) Sunday 15 miles in 2 runs	49
Week 4	Monday 4 miles Tuesday 8 miles Wednesday 10 miles Thursday 4 Miles Friday 8 miles Saturday (Rest) Sunday 15 miles in 1 or 2 runs	49

<u>Week 5</u>	Monday 4 miles Tuesday 8 miles Wednesday 12 miles Thursday 4 Miles Friday 8 miles Saturday (Rest) Sunday 16 miles in 1 or 2 runs	52
<u>Week 6</u>	Monday 4 miles Tuesday 8 miles Wednesday 12 miles Thursday 4 Miles Friday 10 miles Saturday (Rest) Sunday 16 miles in 1 or 2 runs	54
<u>Week 7</u>	Monday 4 miles Tuesday 8 miles Wednesday 13 miles Thursday 4 Miles Friday 10 miles Saturday (Rest) Sunday 18 miles in 1 or 2 runs	57
<u>Week 8</u>	Monday 4 miles Tuesday 8 miles Wednesday 13 miles Thursday 4 Miles Friday 10 miles Saturday (Rest) Sunday 18 miles in 1 or 2 runs	57
<u>Week 9</u>	See week 8	

Week 10	Monday 4 miles Tuesday 8 miles Wednesday 13 miles Thursday 4 Miles Friday 10 miles Saturday (Rest) Sunday 20 miles in 1 or 2 runs	59
Week 11	See week 10	59
Week 12	So 4 miles Monday through to Friday (Rest Saturday) then try the Marathon distance on Sunday	

At no time must you put in any speed work. All the runs must be slow and steady. If you feel the need to walk or rest – do so. If you feel the need to have two rest days – do so. But, if you wish to complete the marathon distance without too much tiredness and discomfort you have got to have consistency in training. However, a couple of days off from time to time will do no harm.

Lightning Source UK Ltd.
Milton Keynes UK
UKOW03f0158101013

218749UK00001B/1/P